"With sensitivity born of her own struggles, Shirin Taber speaks to today's young women calling them to go deeper in their relationship with Christ and find the fulfillment their hearts long for."

—POPPY SMITH, Author of *Wisdom for Today's Woman* and *Speaking Wisely—Exploring the Power of Words*

"Shirin Taber is a girlfriend who cheers you on in the journey toward finding identity, significance, satisfaction, and intimacy in your relationship with Jesus Christ."

—SHERI MUELLER, Co-founder of Growthtrac.com

"Shirin Taber has done her homework. She writes an engagingly direct and honest account of the struggles of today's woman, and she forecasts the struggles of tomorrow's woman. Shirin is practical, authentic, and challenging. I am going to give this book to the women I love."

—JUDY NELSON, Editor in Chief, *Worldwide Challenge* Magazine

---

"Wanting All the Right Things is fabulous! In an incredibly fresh way, Shirin has articulated the inward struggle of today's young woman."

—ANN DUNAGAN, Author of *Hand Commands* and *The Mission Minded Child*

"Taber's is a voice that offers hope for today's overwhelmed young women."

"Wanting All the Right Things *is an important book that describes the strong, cultural influences on women since the 1970s to be independent and career-focused."*

"Wanting All the Right Things *is like a cup of coffee and a long awaited heart-to-heart with a trusted friend. Shirin Taber understands the issues that have been secretly lurking in the hearts of today's women and offers practical ways we can anchor our identity in the unshakable foundation of who we are in Jesus Christ."*

Finding a Spiritual, Balanced, & Fulfilled Life

SHIRIN TABER

[RELEVANTBOOKS]

Published by RELEVANT Books
A division of RELEVANT Media Group, Inc.

www.relevantbooks.com
www.relevantmediagroup.com

© 2006 Shirin Taber

Published in association with the literary agency of Sanford Communications, Inc., 16778 S.E. Cohiba Ct., Damascus, OR 97015.

Design by RELEVANT Solutions
Cover photography and design by Anna Melcon
Interior design by Anna Melcon, Jeremy Kennedy

Library of Congress Control Number: 2006926597
International Standard Book Number: 0-9776167-9-7

For information or bulk orders:
RELEVANT MEDIA GROUP, INC.
100 SOUTH LAKE DESTINY DR., STE. 200
ORLANDO, FL 32810
407-660-1411

06 07 08 09 10 8 7 6 5 4 3 2 1

Printed in the United States of America

To Elena Setareh and Sage Sohaila Taber.
May you shine like the stars in the universe.

Contents

Foreword

There are three versions of Anne Frank's diary. The first: her own—unedited. The second: an older Anne's self-conscious edit of her original. The third: Anne's father's edit of the edit. It is, of course, the third version that most of us have read.

But, which version represents the real Anne Frank? Where is her true voice? In which account does Anne know what she knows and speak what she knows? In which do we encounter—in purest form—the young visionary who not only names the horrors of her time, but excises its meaning for the annals of history?

In many ways, the young Anne Frank represents the next generation of God-seeking women. These are women who love God and are committed to expanding God's reign of truth, justice, grace, and peace. They have had access to more education and information than any generation in history, These are smart, perceptive women who are not afraid to name and question reality. And they have been called for such a time as this.

However, translating this calling into reality has often come at great personal cost. Old systems created to de-voice women still prevail, whether in religious culture or the world at large. Like their mothers, grandmothers, and great-grandmothers before them, scores of twenty- and thirtysomething women have been taught not to know what they know and most certainly, not to speak what they know—all for the sake of preserving the status quo. The cost to God's work has been incalculable.

But a new generation of women is seriously questioning this norm. Moving out of the "either/or" world of modernism, they are expressing an emerging comfort with complexity and seeming contradiction. Refusing to submit to conservative religion's edits on the one hand ("women can't lead"; "women can't be visionaries"), and rejecting the backwash of classic feminism on the other ("women can't be nurturers"; "women have to be men in order to succeed"), these women want to know, speak, and live in ways that preserve what it means to respond fully to God and what it means to be women.

Shirin Taber has given us an intimate look into the struggles this generation faces as it explores the uncharted territory of "both/and." Old solutions—born in extremes—have left us dry, and many of us seek a higher, richer ground of wholeness. We want to speak in our God-given voices and to affirm them as uniquely female. But we want to enlarge the scope of what that word *female* really means—not for ourselves, but to impact God's kingdom in ways our mothers and grandmothers could not even imagine.

Like Anne Frank, this generation of women Christ-followers want all the right things. They want truth, justice, grace, and peace to reign, beginning with their families and extending outward. Let's hope that their story will be lived and told in the original—courageous and fully voiced into a waiting and needy world.

SALLY MORGENTHALER
Trueconversations.com

Acknowledgments

This book is a tribute to all the women who filled in for my mother (Patricia Ann Madani, 1941–1981). Bold, sacrificial, and loving women like Pam McPoland, Barbara MacDonald, Leslie Ferrell, Mary Peterson, Carol Dodds, Debbie Hetschel, Mastaneh Madani, Souri Hedayati, and Emilie Taber, who took an interest in my life, mentored me, prayed for me, and showed me what it is to be an adult female, a co-laborer, a wife, and a mother. We need more women like you in the world!

This book would also not be possible without people like David Sanford, my enthusiastic collaborator and literary agent, as well as Spencer Burke, Cara Davis, Cameron Strang, Corene Israel, and Cameron Madani, who believed in this project from the start and gave me the impetus to write fast and furiously, with three kids and a new puppy under tow.

Thank you, Clyde, for encouraging the writer in me to blossom, flexing when deadlines beckoned, and allowing our children to see their mother blend home life with vocational dreams. And believing with me that their lives will be richer for it!

I am grateful to the young women at the University of Washington, the University of Denver, the Sorbonne, Bogaziçi University, and in cities like Los Angeles, Paris, Tunis, Moscow, Tashkent, Istanbul, and Tehran—women who were the kindling for this book to burn brightly in my heart. I hope this brings more women closer in the end.

Introduction

[Camera is directly overhead. Desperate housewife Gabrielle and her young lover, John, lie intertwined in sateen sheets on her bed. Lying back to back, each stares blindly ahead, contemplating what has just happened. They have obviously just had sex. The camera zooms slowly, framing their faces.]

JOHN:	So ... why did you marry your husband?
GABRIELLE:	Well, he promised to give me everything I've ever wanted.
JOHN:	And did he?
GABRIELLE:	Yes.
JOHN:	So why aren't you happy?
GABRIELLE:	I wanted all the wrong things.

—DESPERATE HOUSEWIVES,
Pilot episode

Apart from the grace of God, I could have ended up on Wisteria Lane with the rest of the desperate housewives. Like nearly 50 percent of my female peers, I could have had an affair, ended my marriage in a divorce, or abandoned my children—whether emotionally or physically—by the time I turned thirty. My secular feminist education had prepared me for the single life. Individualism. A man's world. Like Bree, Gabrielle, Susan, and Lynette, I could have been unlucky in love, desperate for anything that would help me feel as though I had the control and power my generation promised me.

Like many of you, I was groomed for leadership, varsity competition, and honors everything. I believed I had enormous potential. I had freedom of choice and reckless bravery. I remember hearing messages like "You can do whatever boys can do" or "Get a good career, just in case you ever get divorced." I was convinced I could do anything—and should, in fact, do everything—my heart desired. I was born during the sexual revolution, toddled around in Pampers, and rode my Big Wheel in the early 1970s. If Wonder Woman and Charlie's Angels could take on the bad guys, so could I. (I realize if you were born in the 1980s, you just envisioned Cameron Diaz instead of Farrah Fawcett, but believe me, Farrah was quite the feminine icon long before she landed on reality television.)

But then life happened: college, travel abroad, my first apartment, career, and marriage to the man of my dreams. So why did I so often feel a strange mixture of rage and fear? Or, as Judith Warner describes in her book *Perfect Madness*, an existential discomfort? What happened to all the "choices" my feminist forerunners had ushered in a generation before me?

I suddenly realized my choices had taken on a life of their own. Married life looked radically different than single life. If it's true that more than 90 percent of females marry and have children sooner or later, why hadn't anyone prepared me for the inevitable? Feminism had seriously let me down.

I needed new answers to navigate my life as a young wife and mother. My choices had evolved, morphed, or completely disappeared. Some choices didn't even feel like real choices anymore. I quickly realized that I had not prepared myself educationally, emotionally, or spiritually for the realities of life—sharing a bed, mortgage, childcare, and a retirement plan with my husband.

You see, the dirty little lie that I grew up believing is that there's very little difference between men and women. Sure, we get pregnant, feel miserable for nine months, nurse our young—but then we basically go on with our lives.

Right?

Wrong. A woman's life is more complicated than that. According to journalist Peggy Orenstein, who interviewed two hundred women between the ages of twenty and forty for a study, "Women's lives have become a complex web of economic, psychological, and social contradictions, with opportunities so intimately linked to constraints that a choice in one realm can have unexpected consequences (or benefits) ten years later in another."[1] This means the world is half-changed for our generation; we've receive new freedoms and choices, but we also get handed a new set of consequences once we marry and start a family.

At the same time, our anxiety is exasperated by the invasion of media and advertising into our lives, the desire to have the types of careers for which we have been educated, and the lack of role models. We face pressure from a society obsessed with physical appearance, celebrities, and consumerism, as well as the effects of the plastic-surgery and weight-loss industries.[2] No one has taken the time to show our generation how to plan and prioritize for the marriages and families we so desperately want.

While the feminist movement has actually done great things for the voice and value of women, as well as brought discrimination and protection issues to light, it's also perhaps swung the pendulum a little too far in convincing us that anything men can do, we can do better—and then some. The honest truth is that we are not just like men after all. Secular feminism and its answers to finding true female happiness are not expansive enough to cover all the seasons of a woman's life.

So whom do we look to for satisfying answers? The Church, our parents, educators, politicians, the media, Beverly LaHaye and the Concerned Women of America, or Danielle Crittenden and the Independent Women's Forum? Sadly, as a practicing Christian, I have found the Church and conservative women's groups to be ill-equipped in keeping up with rapid societal changes. Many seem divided on the merits and positive aspects of the women's movement, focused still on the backlash of the 1970s' sexual revolution rather than listening to the needs and interests of women today. While a growing number of denominations and theologians—like Rebecca M. Groothuis, author of *Women Caught in the Conflict*—have begun to embrace gender egalitarianism, they aren't providing practical advice for young women who juggle marriages, young children, and vocations.

Traditionalists like Mary Kassian in *The Feminist Mistake* seem to communicate that the sole responsibility of a woman is to be her husband's helper. They offer no discussion regarding a woman's education and intellectual interests. A stay-at-home mom is thus the Excalibur Sword or the antidote to the breakdown of society. While traditionalists advance the "Victorian" family, they leave me wondering if the brand of isolationism they encourage is truly biblical or if it smacks strangely of "hiding our light under a bushel." What about the needs outside of our family? What about domains that call for the representation of a woman's voice? What kind of message are we sending our daughters' generation about their future roles in society and in the Church?

I feel torn, unsure whom to believe and what paths to follow. Meanwhile, our confusion leads us to hyper-manage our domestic lives more than we should and to blame our husbands when things don't turn out as we expect. A yoke of anxiety and guilt weighs us down, making us unpleasant to be around.

———

Researchers are finding that women born between 1958 and 1972 are some of the most frazzled, stressed-out, exhausted, and unsatisfied women in history.[3] These likely include your mother, your older sister, your role models—the people from whom you've learned what it means to be a woman. It is the women in the generation ahead of you that have demonstrated what it looks like to have a career and a husband and a family and a well-appointed home. Like me, you're probably asking yourself, "Is this the kind of life I want?"

All the rah-rah about how great girls are has led today's women to believe we should be nearly superhuman. In fact, we've become perfectionists and expect everyone around us to be perfectionists, too. Our worldview may be driving us over the edge of sanity. In the end we find ourselves out of sync with nature, the men in our lives, the friends we need so desperately, our beloved children, and even God Himself. We end up sacrificing our feminine soul.

———

Unless you are reading this book in a village somewhere in the third world, gone are the days when mothers, cousins, aunts, grandmothers, and female mentors huddled together at the hearth, giving loving and supportive advice about marriage, motherhood, community life, and the pursuit of vocational dreams. Yet we need each other more than ever. Many of us grew up as latchkey kids, come from broken homes, or weren't taught to plan or prioritize for the difficult crossroads we find ourselves facing today. Our baby-boomer mothers and fathers, influenced by the sexual revolution, have in many respects only added to our confusion. They've taught us to mistrust men, become economically self-reliant, indulge our anger, and pursue independence—at any cost.

My story isn't unique. Talk to any woman under the age of thirty-five, and you will likely learn that our generation of post-baby boomers is unsure about how to navigate the pitfalls of living in a culture torn between feminism and traditionalism. The truth is that we want to do all the right things, but we aren't sure how. We ask ourselves: How do we hang on to the positive aspects of feminism and maintain our careers? What traditional values are essential to protect and care for today's family? How do we find the happiness that eludes many modern women? What will we tell our daughters?

Most books that address the anxiety of today's young women come from secular publishers: *What Our Mothers Didn't Tell Us* by Danielle Crittenden, *Perfect Madness* by Judith Warner, *The B---- in the House* by Cathi Hanauer, *Are Men Necessary?* by Maureen Dowd, and *The Beauty Myth* by Naomi Wolf. While these books, written by upper-middle-class Washington insiders, diagnose the insecurity and desperation, young women feel their answers are often political (i.e., longer maternity leave, free childcare, more tax breaks) or down on men. They offer few personal stories and practical suggestions to overcome our bitter predicament. Their secular worldviews do not permit them to address the needs of young women who want their lives to be characterized by integrity, honor, and faith.

Wanting All the Right Things will show you how to face your anxieties and insecurities, and offer real suggestions to live a more satisfying, Christ-centered life. This book will push you to begin planning and prioritizing for the healthy and godly family you long for, instead of succumbing to a stressed-out and control-freakish lifestyle you'll later regret. This is not your mother's book. It's not written for women over the age of thirty-five (though they are welcome to look inside as well). This book describes your life, not the lives of other generations who have come before you.

Stories based on my personal experiences and interviews with college students, young professionals, wives, and mothers both in the United States and abroad will enable you to embrace biblical values as you develop your sense of identity and relationship with God. This book is meant to generate conversation between you and your friends, allowing you to explore private and unspoken feelings, let go of your competitive nature, and enjoy your relationships again.

In the upcoming chapters I will address the seven areas I have found to produce stress and anxiety in young women's lives today. We are desperate for significance, beauty, intimacy, solitude, financial security, a legacy, and the supernatural. While these desires are not inherently wrong, we become stressed out, consumed by rage and fear, when we pursue them in order to feel in control or validated as human beings.

We are a generation of young women who need freedom to work through the issues and practices of marriage, motherhood, vocational pursuits, and life in a community. We are a new group of women whom some call the "third wave" (postmodern and progressive in our views of gender, careers, and domestic life). We don't buy into the Old World, feminist jargon about bra burning and glass ceilings. We know that if we put our minds to something, we can really do it, whether it's becoming a brain surgeon or launching a billion-dollar enterprise. We believe in a new wave of activism for younger women living in the wake of 9/11, the AIDS crisis, and the wars in Afghanistan and Iraq. We want to make a difference in the world.

We follow in the steps of the early feminists at the beginning of the twentieth century and those who revolutionized feminism and the use of birth control in the 1960s and 1970s. But our generation knows new problems have arisen. Our mothers often lived burned-out lives and ended their marriages in divorce. We don't want to make their mistakes. We are looking for new ideas, new paradigms, and new solutions to respond to today's life questions. We are a new wave surging forward. We want our lives to be characterized by a mixture of traditional and progressive ideals—an emerging femininity.

This book will not be directional in scope, but will seek to create a cultural conversation among young women. I want to get readers asking the right questions and making the right choices. I will attempt to show a high view of marriage and motherhood—but not at the cost of dying to our dreams or intellect. This generation intuitively knows from our baby-boomer parents and broken-home experiences that the gods of sex, money, and power don't satisfy. In our hearts we yearn for the Great Story, the cabin at the end of the lake, where happy families congregate for a great feast ... the other side of heaven.

I confess that I still believe the feminist mantra that I can do it all—but that doesn't always mean I should. I occasionally watch a show like *Desperate Housewives* and am entertained by the witty story line, the fashion, or the home décor, but I still thank God at the end of the evening that my life doesn't have to mirror the lives of the characters. By the grace of God I can see how far I have come and pass on to my daughters a heritage of faith and hope. So turn the pages, and let me share with you my personal story of how I awoke one day and began to sense a dark chasm between my reality and my desired identity, and the hope I found on the other side.

Chapter 1

WHAT NO ONE EVER TOLD US

"For women to achieve some kind of balance in marriage, motherhood, and career it seems, for millions of women, as probable as stumbling across the Holy Grail."

—DANIELLE CRITTENDEN,
What Our Mothers Didn't Tell Us

I wish I could've sat down with my mother face to face and learned about the realities of adult female life. All the "training" I've received from her comes from cloudy memories of a mother who was respected by her peers but was insecure and exhausted most of the time. I loved her, and I know she loved me, but our feelings for one another weren't shared openly. Like many of the women of her generation, my mother's marriage was rocky and she had to work to help pay the bills. My dad was gone much of the time because of an international work assignment, and relatives and childhood friends lived far away. We were the quintessential 1970s family—Mom was basically raising three kids on her own, with a limited support system.

Sure, there were those rare quiet moments of intimacy in the car on the way to soccer practice, or buying clothes together for a violin recital, but on the whole, we didn't talk much. Because she carried the lion's share of the work at home and didn't include me in chores beyond cleaning my room, I knew little of her world. I didn't know how she decided what to cook for dinner each night, how she took care of the bills and the family, what books she read, what television programs she liked, or whom she turned to for parenting advice. Everything just seemed to magically happen.

Now that I'm in my thirties and a mother of three, I have many questions. Did she worry about drugs and premarital sex when I entered middle school, the way I worry about my kids? Did she dream about what college I might attend? Did she even expect me to go to college? Did she wonder about the kind of man I might marry?

I didn't know much about her spiritual or emotional life either, except that she didn't take communion at church and that she felt "different"—possibly a threat—among our neighbors since my dad was gone most of the time. I did know she was tired, lonely, and insecure about her appearance, and tried desperately to keep her marriage alive. But these were things I inferred—nothing she ever told me directly. So many secrets. So much left unsaid. And then she died suddenly from leukemia when I was in junior high. The dream of being adored and mentored by a mother was forever gone.

I am not alone. Many of the girls I have talked to over the years, in my work on college campuses and among young professionals, have shared the same kinds of stories. Their mothers may not have died when they were fourteen, but a chasm existed between them nonetheless. Divorce, blended families, alcoholism, work, caring for aging parents, financial problems, church, tennis, decorating ... something always seems to create a barrier to meaningful and authentic relationships between mothers and daughters. So little forethought is given to how we'll turn out as wives and mothers ourselves, and whether or not we'll be truly prepared.

Perhaps feminism created the need for mothers to distance themselves from their daughters, to raise them like boys. After all, the man's world became the standard for female fulfillment—sex, money, and power. We were the generation who "had it all." There were great expectations for us. We'd experience the freedoms and privileges our mother's generation had fought for. As Judith Warner, author of *Perfect Madness*, explains, we were raised to see ourselves as winners. "We'd been bred, from the earliest age, for competition. Our schools had given us co-ed gym and wood-working shop, and had told us never to let boys drown out our voices in class. Often enough, we'd done better than they had in school. Even in science and math. And our passage into adulthood was marked by growing numbers of women in the professions. We believed that we could climb as high as we wanted to go, and would grow into the adults we dreamed we could be."[1]

If my mother were alive today, I'd ask her why the women of my generation—the most liberated and most educated in all of history—feel so competitive toward one another and fearful of never quite measuring up to so many illusionary and make-believe standards. Why do we feel the need to be more beautiful, more successful, or more interesting than everyone else? Why are we so competitive in parenting, in decorating, in staying fit—even in experiencing God?

But these are questions my mother will never be able to answer for me this side of heaven. So I press on and try to

answer them myself, hoping that some of the answers I find
might help others, too.

THE CONFESSIONS OF A DESPERATE HOUSEWIFE

I shouldn't have been watching *Desperate Housewives*. I gave
up television a decade ago when I moved to Europe to become
a university chaplain. Cultural adjustments and parenting two
preschoolers fatigued me too much to waste time in front
of my French tube. Call me pious, but I've continued my
television fast since moving back to the United States five years
ago. I tell myself I have better things to do than get hooked on
shows like *CSI*, *Grey's Anatomy*, or *The Apprentice*. Besides, I
was convinced that *Desperate Housewives* sounded too racy and
pathetic. These women were surely either bedding their tennis
coaches or maxing out their credit cards at Saks Fifth Avenue.
Not my life!

The show piqued my interest, however, when I heard that
series creator Marc Cherry said he wrote the pilot after his
mom revealed to him that she could relate to Andrea Yates, the
Texas mother who drowned her five children in 2001. Cherry
reported in a television press tour that while watching a news
report on Yates, his sixty-seven-year-old mother told him,
much to his surprise, "I've been there."[2]

Call me a hypocrite, but this show hooked me when I
took a peek one night after tucking in the kids, slyly closing
my bedroom doors, and clicking on the television. It was the
episode where Lynette has a vision of blowing her brains out
with a revolver while her four boys run wild like savages,
turning the house upside down. I've never been suicidal, but
that scene riveted me. And I thought to myself, much like
Marc Cherry's mom, *I've been there.*

QUIZ: ARE YOU EXPERIENCING ANXIETY AND INSECURITY ABOUT YOUR IDENTITY?

Sometimes it's helpful to think about where you are in life and what long-term changes you'd like to make. Some may be experiencing more stress than others, but sooner or later we all will, given the world we live in today. Others may be suffering from a roving feeling of discontent with their lives. Place a check mark in front of the statements that describe you.

☐ I feel pressure to look and be perfect all the time. But I secretly feel like I will never measure up.

☐ I wake up in the morning with a list of things to do. I wish I could just sleep in and let someone else take over.

☐ I secretly wish I could be a celebrity and have people adore me. I want to feel recognized.

☐ I wish I had more time to pursue my own personal goals instead of being everyone's caretaker all the time. I am tired of being treated like a maid or picking up after others.

☐ I wish the men at work would take an interest in me and my ideas professionally. I feel undervalued at my job.

☐ I have a hard time containing my anger and blow up more often than I would like. I love my family, but sometimes they bring out the worst in me.

☐ I need more discretionary income to buy clothes, decorate my home, and drive a nicer car. I never seem to have enough money.

☐ I have been told that I can be controlling. I don't mean to; it's just the way I am.

☐ My husband or boyfriend wishes I would be happier and lighten up. I can't help myself. I often find myself angry or on the verge of tears.

☐ I always feel exhausted, like I have no margins in my life for rest and a good night's sleep.

☐ It's hard for me to convey to others what I really want. I feel guilty about expressing my personal needs.

☐ I feel lonely; I wish I had a few close friends nearby. No one seems to notice me.

☐ I have little time to read, pursue hobbies, or exercise when I want. My life feels like a three-ring circus.

☐ I find it difficult to make time to pray or open the Bible. I am often too tired or distracted to spend time with God.

☐ I sometimes feel chest pains or have difficulty breathing.

☐ I am fearful that my kids will fall into the wrong crowd, fail to get into a good college, or lose their faith. I don't want to be a failure as a mother.

☐ I wish I had an older woman in my life to go to with my questions and concerns. Everyone's so busy with their own lives.

☐ I am an overachiever and feel desperate to be validated. I wish people would recognize my work and efforts more.

☐ I wish my husband or boyfriend made more money so I could settle down one day and enjoy motherhood without financial worries.

☐ I feel trapped at home as a mother or in a job I don't feel passionate about. I feel like there's more adventure waiting for me out there, a chance to make a difference in the world, but I am confused about how to move forward.

YOUR SCORE: HOW ANXIOUS ARE YOU?

0-5 You feel good about your life, and the future is looking bright. Share what you learn from this book with friends who struggle more than you do.

6-10 You are experiencing a normal amount of stress, but anxiety is creeping into your life. It's time to address the areas that bring you down before they cloud your world.

11-15 Anxiety is a real part of your life. Some days you feel overwhelmed and desperate for someone to talk to. You need to make more time for yourself before you burn out.

16-20 You may struggle with depression or moments of panic.

You could benefit from a spiritual retreat, more solitude, or exercise. Talk to your husband, a close friend, a pastor, or a counselor about some of your fears and insecurities.

Regardless of your score, chances are this book can benefit you or a friend in need of some perspective. Know that what you are experiencing is normal. Take courage and keep reading.

I recall my snapping point, the morning when I officially joined the *Desperate Housewives* club, the morning that birthed this book. I had dug myself into a dark pit by overcommitting, over-mothering, over-volunteering, and over-controlling the lives of those around me. For a three-month period I was cranky, tired, dictatorial, and eating poorly. It was six o'clock in the morning, and my husband slipped out of bed and tiptoed to the walk-in closet to pull on running clothes for an early morning workout. His movement made a floorboard creak, and I freaked. Like the Wicked Witch of the West, I reared my head out from under the covers and cried, "Don't move! You'll wake the baby! I can't handle it anymore!" Longsuffering as he is, my husband had finally had enough. Having heard these kinds of indignant comments one too many times, he threw up his hands and shot back, "Okay! That's it! I'm calling a marriage counselor this week!"

Thus began my adventure of finally seeing the pressure-cooker existence I had allowed myself to fall into as a millennial woman. I needed to start changing some things in my life: my schedule, my priorities, and the way I related to my family and the world around me. In the following chapters, you will get a chance to learn about my private struggles. It is my hope that they will help you take the steps you need to live the life you want.

No wonder *Desperate Housewives* had such a powerful effect on me. More than twenty-one million people tuned in to the first episode.[3] The show's title evidently struck a chord with many viewers like me. I've since come to learn that *Desperate Housewives* takes a darkly comedic look at suburbia, where the lives of housewives aren't always what they seem. Some say the show's success when it first launched was due in part to the appeal of its characters to real women across the board. Back then, Susan was a divorcée and single mom looking for love. Lynette was a formerly successful businesswoman who struggled as a stay-at-home mother of four unmanageable kids. Bree was the perfect homemaker with a rapidly disintegrating marriage. Ex-model Gabrielle—who should have been happy, since she was married and rich—was having an affair with a seventeen-year-old gardener. And Mary Alice, who chose to mysteriously end it all with a bullet to her head, narrated from the grave.

It was Lynette's character whom I could identify with most. No, not her romping and primping, gossiping, and perfectly coifed hairdos. Lynette was not exactly the best role model, but her display of maternal emotions was the rawest I'd seen on television. I sat there watching, hanging on to her every word, thinking, *I know women like her. I can relate to her.*

Boston Globe writer Ellen Goodman shared my first reaction to the show:

> You have to love this woman [Lynette] struggling to fit her round soul into the square hole of her PTA life. The mom doing the best she can with a mother's little helper from her twins' ADD medication bottle ... It's Lynette who speaks truth to power—the power of the updated and eternal myth of momhood. This "truth" is

that even a woman who purposely chooses to be a full-time mom can be one nap away from losing it. The "truth" is that mothers who would throw their bodies in front of a truck for their children also fantasize about throwing their kids in front of a truck. OK, a little wooden truck.

I have found myself asking why, after forty years of feminism, I so often feel like a desperate housewife. Why do I relate to Lynette? What was it about my upbringing that left me feeling so unprepared and alone in dealing with the stresses of adult female life? Perhaps you are asking the same things.

Because my mom died when I was young, I quickly became independent, even a loner to some extent. Sure, I had friends, but I rarely shared my heart and fears openly. I grew up with the message that I could "choose" what I wanted for my life: a college education, international ministry experience, a career, marriage, children, homeschooling, writing, whatever. But in unexpected ways, my sense of choice and the numerous options afforded to me in modern life have stifled my ability to truly live, to relax and enjoy the moment. Like a mouse caught in an endless maze, I scurry along, looking continuously for the next best thing, never really content, convinced that there has to be some better "choice."

"Have we come full circle to a post-feminine mystique?" Goodman asks. Like many women today, "Lynette is a rare character in the demilitarized zone, talking to both sides. She's saying, yes, you can want to be at home and still admit to going nuts at five o'clock in the afternoon. Yes, you can be fiercely in love with your children and long to pack up the minivan and drive off. Yes, you can be dedicated to doing the right thing and not at all sure you're doing it." While I agree with Goodman, as a Christian I had to raise the question: hasn't

Christ promised us more than this yo-yo female existence? Something was amiss with God's promises, my sanctification, and real life.

FEMINISM VS. TRADITIONALISM

I found myself at a crossroads. My reality and my desired identity felt worlds apart. I started asking myself how I got there and what elements of my upbringing—cultural, academic, or religious—induced these mixed emotions about my life. What triggers bring on the anxiety, the fears, the rage, and the ambivalence?

Certainly, the mixed messages propagated from media and advertising are the most toxic in our times. We can't escape them. They are everywhere—television, radio, the Internet, magazines, shopping malls, grocery store checkout aisles. They permeate our

> *"We are in the midst of a long bumpy era of social change where the relationships between men and women are in flux and marriages may change or end."*[4]
>
> —Ellen Goodman,
> ORLANDO SENTINEL

lives with the oozing message that we are not smart enough, beautiful enough, sexy enough, rich enough, or powerful enough.

The latest wave of feminism (women who came of age in the 1980s and 1990s) embraces the celebration of "girl culture," Riot Grrrls, and "lipstick feminists" obsessed with sex and image as power. The new feminists are cool, smart, skinny, and independent. They are Mischa Barton, Gwen Stefani, Angelina Jolie, Paris Hilton, Jessica Simpson, and the Olsen Twins. Their image is manufactured through the lenses of million-dollar advertisers who want to sell you hair color, jeans, shoes, and handbags.

Spokeswomen for our generation have an increasingly liberal view of their bodies and their sexuality. Young urban, university-educated women are socialized into this consciousness without giving a thought to how their worldview will one day drive them—and all the rest of us—crazy as wives and mothers.

Traditionalists don't offer much help either, rarely showing how faith intersects culture. They seem to communicate that all feminist notions should be resisted. Motherhood has been lifted to an almost godlike status, and the stay-at-home mom is the vaccine against societal breakdown. Think of the pressure this puts on mothers! The "traditional mother" is much in vogue these days. Even Ivy League college students are saying that they plan to quit working as soon as they have a baby.

Don't get me wrong here. I adore my kids and have gone to extravagant ends to educate and raise them. But "much of what is billed today as traditional [mothering] is not really traditional at all," writes theologian Rebecca M. Groothuis in *Women Caught in the Conflict.*[5] The idea that dad is the primary bread winner (and better be making 100K a year) and that mom stays at home and takes care of the kids has little cultural and historical precedent.

In earlier times, parents worked together to educate and raise their children. Mothers worked alongside fathers to run the homestead, and kids had to adjust to their parents' responsibilities (feeding livestock, planting and watering gardens, sewing clothes, grinding wheat, and handwashing laundry)—not the other way around. Women of lesser means worked as seamstresses, tavern maids, housekeepers, and midwives. Historically, mothers didn't have time to be their children's playmates, take them on fun field trips, or homeschool them using the Bob Jones curriculum.

The perceptions we have about motherhood are not necessarily biblical. Much of it was developed in the Victorian era and "revivified in the suburban domesticity of the 1950s," Groothuis says. I'm not knocking the homeschooling movement or trying to breed discontent among stay-at-home moms. Quite the contrary! I'm a stay-at-home mother (who works part-time) and have homeschooled my children. I simply question the extremes my generation has taken to mothering—and the number of women I know living the existence of a walking time bomb.

How did this happen?

As we became a more affluent and industrialized society, mothers had more time on their hands. With the introduction of refrigerators, washing machines, dryers, and store-bought clothes, less time was invested in the chores of running a home, and women began to have more time for other things. Men received status by keeping their wives at home instead of working in a sewing factory or harvesting a field. Married women were encouraged to satisfy their husbands and to train their children to be godly citizens. "The mother's role was defined as to encompass the entire mission of a female's life,"[6] Groothuis says.

Today traditionalists claim a woman's life should focus entirely on her children and home responsibilities once she becomes a mother. But in reality, most young women who call themselves "traditional" have benefited greatly from the feminist movement, even taking many of their freedoms for granted. Sooner or later they will need to acknowledge that one formula will not work for all women. Rather than telling young mothers that they must be the primary caregivers of their children and home-life traditionalists, we would do better to tell them that it is their "right" while encouraging them to find helpful solutions for whatever satisfies them.

Times have changed. Our culture has evolved at lightning speed, and the confines of home often do not entirely satisfy

a university-educated woman. Could it be that in clinging
to a Victorian model, some Christians are acting contrary to
Jesus' words in Mark 7:8: "You have let go of the commands
of God and are holding on to human traditions" (TNIV)?
Are we putting undue pressure on young women today to be
superhuman?

Rather than cursing the darkness, Christians should anticipate
changes in adult female life. Instead of reacting with hostility
and indignation, we should look for new ways to encourage
women to love their families and develop their minds and
souls. Let's teach women how to reach out to their neighbors
and engage in culture. Let's encourage them to use their
education and training—through the arts, media, science,
medicine, and social work—to help the needy, single parents
and the growing number of immigrants and internationals. Let's
make a difference in the world together.

MY JOURNEY

By the time I was a freshman in college, I had made a
personal commitment to follow the teachings of Christ. The
decision came easily—after losing my mom as an adolescent,
witnessing my dad's struggles with unemployment, living part-
time with foster parents, helping raise two younger brothers,
and striving to be a good student and athlete, I began sensing
my need for divine guidance. There was no other place to go
but the cross.

Through the loving encouragement of a neighbor, I began
attending church regularly and found friends who accepted me
and spurred me on in my faith. I got involved with a Christian
group called Campus Crusade for Christ at the University of
Washington and, after graduation, participated in a one-year
missions trip overseas. These were some of the best years of
my life. I blossomed. I began dating. I saw how my unique

background and gifting might be used for Christ. I thought I'd been taught everything I'd need to live a happy, successful life. I had more head knowledge than was good for me.

For me, married life and parenting became the terrain for living out the reality of my faith. After a few years, though, something occurred to me: instead of experiencing joy, peace, and fulfillment from my relationships and commitments, I found that I felt more cranky, tired, and cynical. I fantasized about going to bed at eight thirty and sleeping twelve hours each night. I even wondered if the Christian life was for the birds.

The things I learned in college and at church were not carrying me very far into my adult life as a wife and mother. I had questions about roles—mine, my husband's, and God's. I fretted over boredom at home with three young children, though from an outsider's perspective, I was extremely ambitious. I wanted to write and get more involved in the arts but feared sacrificing the safety and character of my children if I was away too much. The anxiety seeped into my bones.

After watching and hearing about the same patterns in the lives of my female friends, I've come to learn that it helps to identify the areas of my life that make me feel so desperate. Like the characters on *Desperate Housewives*, I can name the things that cause me to feel inadequate, insecure, frantic, and fearful. Bree is a perfectionist homemaker on steroids. Like her, I am desperate for control in my family, anxious to pass on a legacy of dignity and honor to my kids. Like Gabrielle, I'm desperate to feel beautiful and financially secure. Like Susan, I'm desperate for intimacy and adoration by a lifelong partner. And like Lynette, I'm desperate for significance, to feel that my choice to be a stay-at-home mother matters and that I can still have a life outside of the home. These desires are not wrong— in fact, I believe they are mostly God-given. The problem lies more in what we believe will meet those needs.

The irony is that we're told that having a successful career and a perfect body, becoming a perfect mom and wife, and owning a house worthy of HGTV—as well as all the accoutrements of the soccer mom—will earn us security, purpose, contentment, intimacy, and peace. But the irony is that these often breed the opposite—stress, discontent, insecurity, and isolation. Christ's teachings say that we can have those needs fulfilled. They're not gained, however, from what we do or have in life, but rather from how we do it. What matters is the heart, the motivation, and the expectations. Our core needs are met in an intimate relationship with God, bringing Him into our choices and allowing His values and principles to help us live out those choices.

> *"Maybe it's not our lives that we can't afford but our aspirations, the things we were brought up to believe we could get from life."[7]*
>
> —Sandra Tsing Loh,
> ATLANTIC MONTHLY

Jesus said, "Come to me, all you who are weary and burdened, and I will give you rest. Take my yoke upon you and learn from me, for I am gentle and humble in heart, and you will find rest for your souls. For my yoke is easy and my burden is light" (Matt. 11:28–30, TNIV). I'm not saying life won't be hard and challenging. That's a promise. But it's through those hard, challenging seasons that we learn and grow to trust God. As we allow Christ, rather than the mixed messages of feminism and traditionalism, to navigate our lives, we learn that He can help us make the best choices in every realm of life. We don't have to live a frazzled, stressed-out, exhausted, and unsatisfied existence.

I'm identifying more than ever with the words of Danielle

Crittenden when she says, "The problem we face as modern people—and particularly as modern women—is how to reconcile the old with the new. Young women today have to confront the daunting task of trying to plan their lives from scratch, with very little in the way of guidance about how to reconcile their modern ambitions with old institutions of marriage and motherhood."[8]

She goes on to say that finding solutions for women's problems will require new ways of thinking about our lives. "To do that, we must begin accepting that our problems originate not in our oppression (as militant feminists would want us to believe) but in our new freedoms." The freedoms we've gained are fantastic undertakings, but to enjoy them we must not be conquered by them. We must learn to think about our preconceived assumptions when we come to a roadblock. It means looking back at what we have given up for what we now possess.

I know that I, for one, tend to assume that my problems arise from inequality in my marriage or some form of sexism. I catch myself thinking, *If only I could get out from under my "husband's thumb," make a little more money, and have a little time to myself, I'd find more happiness.* But if I'm going to overcome my problems, my exhaustion, my need for financial security, I must take these problems to God rather than resent my spouse when I feel overwhelmed. God's there for me and ready to help me.

I first learned about my "feminine soul" while traveling and living overseas. I spent a year in Istanbul, Turkey, after I graduated from college. In countless teahouses and living rooms, I discovered that Eastern women—yes, even in oppressed, uneducated third-world countries—seem more comfortable with womanhood. They're more comfortable with their bodies, their babies, their men, their female relationships, and even their vocations, which are frequently limited to motherhood or part-time employment. During my travels to places like the Middle East, North Africa, and Europe, I observed women from various cultural, economic, and educational backgrounds who seemed more at peace with their feminine identity than we do in our modern and secular Western world.

Surprised?

In many respects, these women from ancient cultures come from traditions and customs similar to the teachings of the Bible. The manner in which they gracefully move from domestic life to professional life amazes me. Relationships seem to always outweigh schedules and timelines. Great value is placed on the art of hospitality and serving your loved ones. They are simultaneously stylish and modest. My friends there often comment that Americans seem hurried, obsessive, aloof, and more goal-focused than relationship-focused. And to be brutally honest, I have to agree with their observations. Their comments represent my own life, as well as that of my peers, much of the time.

So I'm working on developing my feminine soul. It's not easy when you've been raised like a boy most of your life, but I know she's there somewhere. I'm watching other women, listening more carefully, asking lots of questions, and looking for mentors. I have my radar on, and I'm taking mental notes. I hope you'll do the same as a result of reading this book.

I'm praying and taking steps to stop my "split-personality" behaviors—exercising my feminist muscle when I feel like I need more control or playing the "spoiled princess" when I want my husband to provide for me instead. This requires the Holy Spirit's infusion into my life. I need to admit my need for the Spirit at all times. I must consciously depend on God's power source in order to be the woman I need to be. As Crittenden shares:

> The solution lies in the ultimate rejection of politics
> as the solution to one's personal problems. It lies
> in honestly reassessing our desires as women. It lies
> in truthfully acknowledging the sacrifices we have
> made in exchange for our current freedoms. It lies
> in rethinking the ways we arrange our lives. And
> it lies, maybe most of all, in a readiness to reach a
> rapprochement with men—one based on mutual
> respect for each other's difference, but also upon the
> mutual recognition of how much we need and desire
> each other.[9]

I'm learning, and I hope you will too, that Christ can give us the dreams of our hearts. We can overcome the yo-yo existence of a desperate housewife. In the following pages I will share with you my personal stories and interviews with friends who have either graduated or have nearly graduated from a "desperate housewives" existence. Together we will explore seven areas that make us, post-baby-boomer females, feel desperate, frantic, anxious, or joyless. I want to give you hope, not the dreary picture of female existence painted on the cover of *Cosmopolitan*. We'll look at helpful solutions to move beyond a desperate life to an authentic one. Not all areas I address may ignite such a desperation in you, but it may be helpful to you in your sphere of relationships with other women who struggle in their own ways. Use this book to strengthen your identity and to help others do the same. Turn the page and take a look at a desperate housewife's journey to greater levels of freedom and the assurance that I am living the life I am meant to live.

Chapter 2

DESPERATE FOR SIGNIFICANCE

"We are living in an age of such incredible competition and insecurity—financial insecurity, job insecurity, life insecurity—that it often feels as if you have to run twice as fast just to stay relatively, securely in place."

–JUDITH WARNER,
Perfect Madness

I have an insatiable need to feel extraordinary, to be a woman of influence, and to leave a mark on the world. Some might say it's because I grew up as a "third-culture kid," a global nomad. By that, I mean I'm a blend of two cultures—the daughter of an American mother and an Iranian father who lived for five years in the Middle East as a child. My family traveled the world with my father's exciting international airline career. I spent time in cities like Rome, Frankfurt, London, Tehran, and New York and attended a bilingual, private British school before the age of ten. On top of that, Iranians have a unique way of looking at the world through "royal" lenses. An outsider may observe that we behave like little kings and queens. We can't help it. We're poets, artisans, writers, painters, musicians, architects, and gourmet cooks who once ruled a dynasty called the Persian Empire. It's in my blood, and I'm desperate for significance.

Many of my peers—girlfriends, college students, and young professionals I have worked among—are feeling the growing itch for significance too. They want to know they matter and that their life has a purpose. They want to help change the world for good, not just watch from the sidelines. I hear it in the way young women talk about their dreams and vocational aspirations. "I want to open a shelter for poor and disenfranchised women." "I want to make movies like Steven Spielberg." "I want to be a neurosurgeon." We believe our God-given destiny is where our greatest happiness lies.

Gone are the days when eighteen-year-olds went off to college to find a man, had two or three kids, and settled for a predictable life in suburbia. We want to feel like individuals, unique and set apart. Many of us embody a mixture of bohemian and bourgeois ideals, seeking to find our distinguished space in the universe. We like to try new things, we've created our own blogs, and we wouldn't think twice about moving across the country to do medical research, pursue the big screen, go into politics, help with relief work, or teach inner-city kids. Sure, it would be great to marry our college sweetheart, but many young women have places to go and things to do.

For my twenty-seven-year-old aspiring filmmaker friend, Naji, significance is feeling and knowing that she's doing what God has called her to do and dreaming big, even if others may write it off as nothing more than just a dream. It's also getting the recognition, she says, "that who I am and what I do does and will make a difference in the world, even after I'm gone." As a follower of Christ, she wants to be part of God's history. And for her that means making provocative and inspiring films.

Perhaps it's also our obsession with celebrities and powerful people that compels us toward celebrity status. After learning our ABCs on *Sesame Street*, we're saturated every waking moment by success stories and the lifestyles of the rich and famous via the television, Internet, advertising, and gossip magazines. We want to be stars too. We're a generation desperate for significance. For good or bad, it propels us forward, making us breathless for influence, desirous to have our voices heard.

> WOMEN OUTNUMBER MEN AS LAW-SCHOOL DEANS, FILL 30 PERCENT OF MBA SLOTS AT TOP SCHOOLS, MAKE UP 46 PERCENT OF THE LABOR FORCE, AND OWN 48 PERCENT OF PRIVATELY HELD FIRMS.[1]

My husband would tell you he fell in love with me because of my "rugged, sacrificial spirit." I'd call it a spirit for dramatic adventure and for anything outside the traditional box. Mix in the fact that I'm a little bit of an adrenaline junkie, too. I studied Marxism and early Church history, and I got stoked by the idea of working in exotic and dangerous places like the former Soviet Union (during the Cold War era) and Istanbul, Turkey. My time in those countries only convinced me of greater possibilities.

After I married my husband, we moved to Paris for several
years to work with international college students as university
chaplains. I loved working with young people and wanted
to be where the action was. Paris seemed like the coolest
destination in my eyes. Sipping strong coffee on Boulevard
Saint-Germain with future economists, geneticists, theologians,
and philosophers captivated me. I also took advantage of the
time to teach my young children about the world's finest art at
the Louvre and history by visiting chateaus on the weekends.
Life couldn't have felt richer for a woman enraptured by
greatness.

When I was a college student back in the late 1980s, only a
handful of students ventured out, despite their parents' fears, to
spend an entire year overseas. Today students are leaving the
comforts of home to help change the world en masse. Brave
women are going off to fight the war in Iraq, heading to Siberia
as missionaries, backpacking their way through India as relief
workers, and teaching English in China. Girls are going where
they've never gone before. And why wouldn't we? We were
bred to believe we can do anything, go anywhere—even if it
might cost us our lives. Gender no longer holds us back. But is
there a dark side to our drive, our need to achieve, shine, and
even outdo others?

To be honest, my hunger for significance is deeply rooted in
a desperate need to feel valued and validated as a young woman
from a broken home with a nominal religious upbringing.
Perhaps you've felt like you've been there, too. My drive is an
attempt to create an identity from scratch. My parents loved
me but didn't take the time to speak to my heart, to tell me
who I was, to give me a legacy. Based on my work among

college women and young professionals, I will venture to say that the drive for significance in many young women today is rooted in the desperation to feel known and to know that our lives count. We're not just significance addicts, after all. We're hoping that if we can keep up with the big boys, then we are truly worthwhile and interesting.

On another level, I need to admit that my obsession with success is a cry for attention, security, and, ultimately, the need for spiritual healing. I need my heavenly Father to show me that I matter to Him. The broken and missing parts still need to be restored. I long for affirmation and validation that I am loved. When parents don't tell their children that they love them, they will look for other relationships and experiences to speak to their aching hearts. The significance-shaped vacuum cries out and seeks the comfort of the world's applause.

One of the negative byproducts of living in an affluent society is that I'll never completely feel significant. Someone will always seem smarter, richer, or more beautiful. The media constantly bombards me with the message that I don't measure up. I always need some new gadget, beauty product, or degree to make me feel good about myself. I'm up when I feel skinny like a fashion model, but down when my home doesn't look like the cover of a Pottery Barn catalog. I'm elated when my writing gains the approval of a literary agent or publisher, but deflated when I'm not publicly recognized for launching a new media project at work. Up, down. Down, up. My significance barometer can be as erratic as a pogostick.

SOMETHING'S GOT TO GIVE

Something happened in my thirties. I suddenly thought, *I've got to do something really big with my life.* As if being a mother of three young children, living overseas, working among some of the best students in the world, and helping my husband kick-start a successful film festival weren't enough. My significance-shaped vacuum was more expansive than I could have imagined!

I needed to do something—something on the scale of starting a multimillion-dollar company, writing a successful screenplay, or building a national library. Given my limited financial resources, and with three kids under the age of eight, I knew I had to work within my means and my priority to be a stay-at-home mom. So I decided to start writing. I didn't want to write just for the sake of writing. I wanted to be a published author. The maniacal drive for significance was surging at an all-time high.

It also helped that I was surrounded by creative and encouraging friends. Just a year earlier, my husband and I had helped launch the Damah Film Festival, a short-film festival that explores spiritual themes.[2] I was suddenly immersed in a culture where anything was possible artistically, as long as you had enough tenacity, faith, and thick skin. So I went for it. I started writing my first novel and completed the first manuscript in thirteen days over Christmas break while my husband entertained the kids. I remember listening to U2's "Elevation," drinking a lot of coffee, and writing. As Stephen King says,

> *"When we refuse to dream beyond our own greed to the world's greatest needs, our boundaries get smaller and smaller, we get farther and farther away from God and tether ourselves to a stake of No Risk."*
>
> —Kathy Peel,
> DISCOVER YOUR
> DESTINY

"Write, write, as fast as I can, you can't catch me I am the Gingerbread Man!"[3]—and I did just that.

Astonishingly eye-opening, I learned in those thirteen days that if I really put my heart into something, even as a young mother, I could do it. I could write a short novel at Flash Gordon speed. And not just any novel, but one that many friends enjoyed reading, giving me the impetus to keep writing and launch my literary career a year later with my first published book, *Muslims Next Door*. It didn't end there. For a book of its genre, *Muslims Next Door* went on to receive exciting media attention, excellent reviews in syndicated newspapers around the country like the *Los Angeles Times*, *The Seattle Times* and the *Detroit Free Press*. *Christianity Today* nominated it for the 2005 Book Award. The *Detroit Free Press* selected it as "one of the top ten spiritual books of the year." And then more newspaper and magazine articles, an honorable mention in *Publishers Weekly*, radio interviews, a cable television appearance, a book signing at Borders, and a lecture in front of eight hundred at Biola University. Ah, the sweet taste of significance!

Others find joy in launching their vocations, even on a very part-time basis, in the realms of fashion, science, media, ministry, or academia. There comes a time in many women's lives, whether they're single or married with children, twenty-three or forty-three, when they instinctively know they're destined for something great—and when the turning point comes, they seize it with a vengeance. Vera Wang, senior editor of *Vogue* and design director for Ralph Lauren, put it this way: "I knew what world I wanted to be in, but wasn't sure I could break into that world. I wanted something to do with fashion. I would have done anything. I would have licked envelopes. I just wanted to be part of it. By the time I was twenty-three, I was senior editor, and then I became European editor for the American *Vogue* in Paris."[4] And I'm thinking, *Can it get any better than that?*

You may not know her name, but Vera Rubin was the mother of a newborn when she presented her findings on the galactic spin to the American Astronomical Society in Philadelphia in 1964. Her work eventually led to the discovery of dark matter. Because she was a new mother, the chairman of her department said he thought he should share the results and wanted to put his name on her paper. Rubin refused, despite the fact that she had no female role models or classmates to support her, and the headlines in *The Washington Post* read, "Young Mother Finds Center of Creation."[5]

Not only passionate for significance but for the significant, Elizabeth Dole, speaking at the National Religious Broadcasters Convention, reflected on what she described as the "three distinct missions" of her life at the Capitol.

> As Secretary of Transportation, I was overseeing our highways, airways, and railways, enhancing safety in each of these venues ... As Secretary of Labor, my priority was American's human resources—improving skills in the work force ... And at the Red Cross, my focus is on inner resources—inspiring people to sacrifice their time, to volunteer, to help others in need, to give their blood and their financial resources to aid the hurting and the dispossessed across America and around the world. I know you can identify with that passion, that sense of mission ... the knowledge that God has called you to a particular vocation or to a volunteer position to serve Him and to serve others to the best of your ability. It's a challenge, but also a great blessing.

Here is a woman who committed her time, talents, and treasures to things that have eternal value—human beings. As women, we have an amazing desire to want to help people, to devote our best energies and finest creative powers to things that make a difference in the world—things that are noble, life-giving, and inherently good for humankind.

THE DARK SIDE

The dark side of a need for significance is the anxiety and desperation it can suddenly bring to our lives when things don't turn out as we expect. We can drive ourselves and everyone around us crazy when we fixate furiously on "our plans and goals." If you're like me, you want to see results right away. You want instant gratification, and you want everyone to love your ideas, to open doors for you, and to treat you like a queen. Sound familiar?

You don't want to publish one book; you want to publish a dozen! Okay, that might just be me, but studies do show our generation is prone to perfectionism.[6] Just read about the stress of trying to be perfect all the time in *Cosmopolitan*,

> "I think my career has been unconventional, but maybe all women's careers are unconventional."
>
> —Vera Rubin, ASTRONOMER

Harper's Bazaar, or *Marie Claire*. Stress sells, says Myrna Blyth, the author of *Spin Sisters* and former editor of *Ladies' Home Journal*. The media and advertising world knows this and plays on our insecurities, our tendency toward perfectionism, and our need to feel sexy, smart, and powerful.

The Sistine Chapel wasn't built in a day. Anxiety begins to rear its ugly head in our lives when "we can't have it all." We lose our joy when we find that we can't manage everything—

timelines to fulfill, limited finances, baby-sitting needs, a house to clean, kids to carpool, homework to check, and dinner to have hot and ready by six o'clock.

I get overwhelmed when I start to believe that I need to prove myself, and I find myself saying things like, "I told my friends I was going to get published, so by golly, I better get published!" Don't be surprised when your drive for significance deteriorates into selfish ambition, greed for success, the adulation of peers, and a cry for validation.

YOUR BEST ENEMY

Every woman who dreams of a life of significance must learn to live with criticism. It's the dreary reminder that we don't have the Midas touch. If we are going to see our dreams become a reality, we must develop the ability to receive criticism and respond properly. This is where determination and thick skin come in.

I'm learning that when I'm faced with the reality that I may not see my dreams fulfilled, or when I feel attacked or disregarded by others who "just don't get" what I am after, I need to take my feelings to God. Philippians 4:6 says, "Do not be anxious about anything, but in every situation, by prayer and petition, with thanksgiving, present your requests to God" (TNIV). I go to God in prayer and say, "Here I am, God. I want to be used by You. I want to effect positive change in the culture around me. I know You can speak through me. Please use me for Your kingdom purposes."

Tenacity is sticking with an idea or project until it's completed—being bull-headed, ruthlessly stubborn about fulfilling your dreams, afraid of no one but God. One of the attributes I've noticed about highly accomplished people is that they finish what they begin and don't give up easily. They make goals and stick to them doggedly while remaining loyal to their vision and to the people they love.

I remember spending some time alone with God one day and charting out a one-year plan to write toward publication. I was inspired by Luke 14:28–30: "Suppose one of you wants to build a tower. Won't you first sit down and estimate the cost to see if you have enough money to complete it? For if you lay the foundation and are not able to finish it, everyone who sees it will ridicule you, saying, 'This person began to build and wasn't able to finish'" (TNIV). I looked at my schedule, my family's needs, and my community responsibilities, and then prioritized writing into my life. I decided to say no to nonessentials. I got in the "zone" and wrote at every opportunity. I wrote in between diaper changes, laundry, homeschool lessons, cooking, grocery shopping, and everything else a mother has to do. Thirteen months later, I signed my first writing contract.

LEARNING TO TRUST GOD

As I grow in my relationship with God and sense His enduring commitment to me, I see that His plans for me are greater than anything I could have imagined. In my twenties I jumped at every opportunity that brought me the thrill of adventure, without necessarily calculating what God had designed me to do as an individual. If something seemed meaningful and helped others, I went along for the ride. As I age and care for my family, I need to trust God to show me what I am uniquely gifted to do. I only have so many hours in the day to devote to a vocation outside the home. But the longing for significance continues to burn brightly.

God hears my cry for significance and whispers, "I put those longings in your heart because I have plans for you. I gave you that voracious hunger for greatness and beauty and purpose because I'm calling you to serve *Me* and reveal *My* marvelous purpose." He is a generous and willing Father who tells His children, "Ask me, and I will make the nations your inheritance, the ends of the earth your possession" (Ps. 2:8, TNIV). He tells me that I'm part of His family, "a chosen people, a royal priesthood, a holy nation, God's special possession, that [I] may declare the praises of him who called [me] out of darkness into his wonderful light" (1 Pet. 2:9, TNIV). As I step out in faith and take hold of the opportunities He gives me, I can trust that He will enable me to leave a lasting influence on the world.

What about women who long to make their lives count but prefer to be behind the scenes? Some dislike or are scared to death of the limelight. They don't have a need to hear their own voice in public or see their name in lights. Can they really make a difference if they're not holding a microphone in their hands and interviewing the presidents of the world, or raising millions of dollars to build an AIDS ministry in Africa? What does humble significance look like to God, and how does He measure it?

Recently my eight-year-old daughter, Elena, told me she was writing a report about Mother Teresa for school. I was touched to think she had picked such a humble figure, a woman who I once heard preferred to clean toilets at an orphanage than publicly receive the praises of men. I knew Mother Teresa had done much to serve people, but somehow her life affected me more powerfully when I read about her in my daughter's handwriting.

Children have a wonderful way of communicating what's most essential, and in the fewest words possible. For Elena, what counted most about Mother Teresa's life was that "she cared for the poor and was unprejudiced toward people of other cultures and religions. She loved and served all in the name of Christ." Mother Teresa once said, "I am a little pencil in the hand of a writing God who is sending a love letter to the world." She had a humble desire to do God's will, and that attracted the world to her. Even Muslims and Jews sang her praises. She orchestrated a ministry of a thousand nuns who operated nearly three hundred centers around the world. There was virtually nothing about her that caused people to question her motives or wonder if she was hungry for fame. I wish I could be more like her. To see her is to understand the word *saint*.

God's word seems clear: humility is something He values in His children, even those who want to do great things. He wants us to think big but keep our heads small:

> **PSALM 25:9** "He guides the humble in what is right and teaches them his way."

> **PROVERBS 11:2** "With humility comes wisdom."

> **PROVERBS 15:33** "Humility comes before honor."

> **MATTHEW 23:12** "Those who humble themselves will be exalted."

> **1 PETER 5:5** "Clothe yourselves with humility toward one another."

Amy, a young professional in Washington, D.C., felt the bitter disappointment of an unrealized dream. Though the experience, which lasted more than two years, was painful, she put her trust in something greater than herself.

> It took a decision on my part to commit my life to serving God full-time in ministry, and a decision on His part not to have me follow through, to understand that even the noblest of vocations can carry selfish intentions.
>
> My weakness was revealed in my reliance on my role as "missionary" to feel significant, to believe that I was holy and pleasing to God. I had never truly trusted that who I was and where I had come from (through Christ's saving grace) were enough to make me significant.
>
> Once I realized that God did not plan for me to be a missionary (by keeping the doors firmly closed), I was crushed. And in some sense, I am still recovering from the loss. Now I am learning that my significance does not lie in the title of being a "missionary"—it lies in Him alone.

Regardless of the cause, many of us will suffer disappointment sooner or later when our plans or dreams aren't fruitful. Society's obsession with winning sets us up for this kind of heartache. The key is to not allow feelings of failure to drive a wedge between you and God. He simply requires a spirit of humility and willingness to be led to the door He wants to open for you (Matt. 7:7–8).

DOES THIS SHOE FIT?

I am married to an ambitious man, and, as you may be

able to tell by now, I am a fairly ambitious woman. One
of the things I struggle with in marriage is my need to feel
significant just as strongly as my husband does. It can leave me
feeling unwomanly at times, like
Cinderella's stepsister who can't
quite squeeze the glass slipper on
her size-ten foot. Either my feet
or my ego are too big. Today's
female ambition is a quirky thing.

> *"Massive professional
> ambition is incompatible
> with massive parental
> ambition."*
>
> —Judith Warner,
> *PERFECT MADNESS*

In hindsight, I probably should
have married a Type B personality
who'd love being Mr. Mom and
joyfully let me fulfill my career
fantasies. Instead, I married a Type A, extremely talented and
industrious baby boomer who'd gleefully work one hundred
hours a week and travel one hundred days out of the year
if I let him. He can't help it. Like me, he loves people and
impacting the world. So we have to address this need for
mutual significance in our marriage on a regular basis.

It's not always easy for him to be a post-feminist male. He
married a strong, independent woman. According to writer
Sam Allis, post-feminist males are just as confused and angry,
desperately seeking manhood. They are also fatigued by trying
to "accommodate" and live up to the performance standards
of the women in their lives. Modern man is not only trying
to form his own sense of identity, but is unlikely to get much
support from his wife, because she is doing much the same.[7]

Working couples must fight against the tendency toward
chauvinism, says Father Daniel O'Connell, a Jesuit priest and
chair of the psychology department at Georgetown University.
When a wife becomes abrasive in her quest for significance, to
prove herself vocationally, she may become guilty of the very
chauvinism she objects to by competing with her man on his

own turf. And "this makes it impossible for a man to show gentleness and reverence for women."[8]

My husband is successful in his work outside of the home. For an ambitious wife, this can cause tension in the marriage. I had to learn to plan and prioritize with my husband rather than dropping things in his lap and getting ticked when his schedule was too full to allow him to help me with my own plans or with childcare. Fortunately, he's open-minded, organized, and helps me anticipate situations where we'll need to work together instead of reacting to the demands of vocational and domestic life.

In recent years, we have been meeting on Saturday mornings for breakfast at a local diner to discuss our schedule and goals. We look at the calendar together, sometimes three months out, and determine when I need more help domestically because of writing projects, deadlines, or a speaking engagement that requires travel. At the same time, I am open to playing hostess and entertaining people who are important to his work. He values that effort. Additionally, I stay supportive when he needs to work late hours and travel internationally.

In *Women Caught in the Conflict,* Rebecca Groothuis shares about her relationship with her husband: "Mutual decision-making is the surest way to hear from God so that we will obey His will for our lives. In a marriage between two people who love and submit to one another, policy of mutual, rather than hierarchical, decision-making is more likely to produce not only harmony among family members, but decisions which are best for all concerned."[9] When we take the time to anticipate the vocational opportunities ahead of us, we find that we enjoy working together as a team, as best friends, rather than jealously competing for a chance to be king or queen of the hill.

CHOOSING LOVE IN THE ALL THE WRONG PLACES

I often share with highly ambitious single women something that feminists or their education never prepares them for: the more powerful a man they marry, the more of a struggle it will be to pursue many of their own personal dreams once kids come along. In marriage, two powerful people are like oil and water. The more successful women become, the more of a threat we are to the men in our lives. Like I said, we're a generation that sees ourselves as winners! This can produce anxiety when the need to feel significant is just as strong for the wife as it is for the husband. I've seen marriages disintegrate when the woman can't reconcile her husband's success with her own need for recognition and achievement beyond the home. Whose dreams come first? Whose schedule needs to bend the most? Who gets to sleep in after a late-night project? Who must postpone dreams and ambitions until the kids are in school full-time?

> "I think of Tracy Chapman's lyrics, 'I don't want no one to squeeze me ... they might take away my life. I just want someone to hold me and rock me through the night.' I relate to this. If I let a man get close enough to hold me, I might not be able to have the life I've dreamed of. I want to make this life count. I want to see and experience the world firsthand, have great adventures, and engage deeply in meaningful service to the eternal Lord during my brief days on this earth."
>
> —Jill Schrag,
> MEDIA PRODUCER

Couples who are highly ambitious are usually drawn to each other because they love the energy and excitement of being together. They respect and push each other forward. But when children come along, that same energy and drive can work against them. Their marriage can turn into a tug of war and competition field. The husband may suddenly want the wife to be more maternal and focus on home life, epitomizing the kind of mother he longed for as a child. The wife may feel more financial fears and be afraid of losing her footing and respect in the professional world.

These insecurities and the stress of caring for young children while pursuing demanding careers can drive an ambitious couple apart rather than bring them together. While the addition of children creates a new level of love in a marriage, it can also test a couple's priorities. Their needs are unpredictable and often exhausting. Most working couples are unprepared for the reality of life with children, and this puts a strain on their relationship. Core fears and convictions can turn the marriage upside down, causing the couple to reassess their commitment level or marital roles. In the end, many think it's better to parent alone than compete with their spouse for more freedom and their own vocational dreams.

Who's at fault? The wife? The husband? Who should be the primary child-care provider? For me, it's important to be with my kids at home when they are young. I am lucky to have a husband who supports this desire and is able to help make this arrangement work for us. But it's not this way for all couples. I can't provide answers or prescribe a formula that works for every man and woman.

Each family's needs vary. I know of situations where the wife must work because her husband is unemployed, ill, or depressed. Some live in expensive areas like Chicago, Los Angeles, and New York, where it's almost impossible to survive on a single income. Others need to work or volunteer because it breathes life into them and makes them better wives and mothers. In the end, women are divided in what our domestic and vocational lives should look like.

But you need to anticipate the tensions on the horizon, the half-changed world of modern women. Whether you are single, married with no kids, or have children, you need to anticipate the day when you and your partner must negotiate the terms of your vocational aspirations—expressing your God-given gifts. You'll need to decide who does what and when. You'll need to decide how you are going to blend your professional and domestic responsibilities.

To enter marriage clueless of such potential tensions and the reality that women are going to want more in life than a couple of kids and a nicely decorated house may be naïve and shortsighted. Sooner or later, you may be clamoring to have your voice heard, to make a difference in your community and in your church, to become an entrepreneur, go back to school, and leave your mark on the world. In a *Newsweek* article titled "Smart Moms, Hard Choices," Peg Tyre reports that 80 percent of mothers are employed or looking for work by the time their kids are twelve.[10] According to Kathleen Gerson, a New York University sociologist, that means only a small percentage of women—usually wealthy ones—can afford to stay at home full-time.

Young couples are looking at their options differently, too. They have grown up around working women, so they are going into relationships assuming they can both work as the need arises. Young women are equipping themselves so that if something ever happens to their husbands and they can no longer provide, the women can find work immediately. So start planning now. Know who you are, and be honest with the people around you.

I hope you will realize your dreams for significance—to become a woman of influence and allow your accomplishments to be driven by eternal kingdom purposes. God is aware of our generation's unique circumstances, needs, desires, and abilities to intersect and transform the culture around us. Instead of being frazzled and anxious to feel significant, let's focus our best energies on the things that really matter in life. If it's a toss-up between relationships and materialism, choose relationships. Anticipate the anxiety and stress that come with modern life, and serve your family and the people you love. Find godly and wise mentors who are seeing the fruit of their hard labor, and don't give up the hope that God has destined us to live an extraordinary life.

Tiffani married her high-school sweetheart, who now mentors successful businessmen, and is a devoted mother of two preadolescent boys in Southern California. In addition to her commitment to her family and church, Tiffani is an executive producer for the interactive DVD titled *JESUS: Fact or Fiction*, which has sold nearly a million copies. An extremely talented woman, Tiffani, like many mothers, questions how to find the right balance in living a life fully surrendered to God and her family, and developing her personal passions. Recently she shared with me:

> I had to learn once again to be satisfied in the day-to-day stuff and recognize the significance my life has in just doing that because with God, it's no less important doing laundry and dishes than creating a multimedia DVD. But I find that hard to do sometimes. As a Type A personality, always maxing out every minute and going for it, I sometimes feel more significant through "actions" than when I work on my character and raise my family ... no brainer. I seem to always want to do things for God rather than just be with God. I'm learning, however, that my life is significant when I am sensitive to the opportunities God gives me each day and see them as divine appointments. For me, living a

life of significance is abiding daily in the Lord, whether through the simple, routine tasks of running a home or something out of my comfort zone, when I experience the thrill of depending on God so much I can easily see and feel Him guiding me.

Like Tiffani, perhaps we all need to learn a little more about yielding our lives and abiding in God's will. Significance is measured by a humble heart, surrendered to God's purposes and willing to say, "Here I am, God. Use me today in a way that reveals Your marvelous love and power to the world around me. It's doesn't have to be glamorous; just use me. I am available." Let's be authentic about our dreams and passions, surrendering the results of our labor to God and never forsaking His children as we reach for the stars.

SIX SECRETS TO CREATING A LIFE OF SIGNIFICANCE

1. WHEN YOU FEEL LIKE YOU ARE BUTTING YOUR HEAD AGAINST THE WALL, ASK YOURSELF: "Am I doing this because it's a worthy and noble cause, or because I have something to prove to the world?" If you have something to prove, drop it.

2. RESEARCH AND EXECUTE. If you're going to do something of lasting value, make sure you know what you are getting into. Whether it's starting a small business, writing a novel, or opening a shelter for pregnant teenagers, make sure you speak to as many experts as possible. Count the financial cost and make sure your personal and family life can accommodate your vocational goals. Then go for it!

3. DEVELOP THICK SKIN. Take criticism lightly, unless you are headed for financial disaster or family problems. Listen to good advice and discard the rest. Plan on feeling anxious and stressed out at times, because that's natural. But then move on.

4. ALWAYS KEEP THE CREATOR INVOLVED IN THE CREATION PROCESS. Listen to His soft whispers of encouragement or correction. Take regular time to pray, reflect, read the Scriptures, and invite God to guide you and open the right doors.

5. AVOID SELFISHNESS OR AMBITIOUS GREED. Money and worldly success never satisfy long-term. A nicer home and fancier cars don't deliver. Let your dream, God's call in your life, compel you toward leaving a significant impact on the world.

6. HAVE FUN! Don't take yourself so seriously that you miss opportunities to make new friends, serve and enjoy people, mentor younger women, play with your kids, or buy yourself a pair of shoes at Nordstrom. Deadlines and opportunities will always be there. "Therefore do not worry about tomorrow, for tomorrow will worry about itself. Each day has enough trouble of its own" (Matt. 6:34, TNIV).

Chapter 3

DESPERATE FOR BEAUTY

"When a woman is forced to adorn herself to buy a hearing, when she needs her grooming in order to protect her identity ... that is exactly what makes beauty hurt."

—NAOMI WOLF,
The Beauty Myth

You know the kind of girls I'm thinking of. They're preppy, dedicated students by day and cruise the club scene by night. These friendly and outspoken millennial girls outperform boys and always look polished, and then at night they put on the skimpiest clothing possible, like Victoria's Secret models in designer jeans and stilettos.

They get 800s on their SATs, are presidents of their class and model UN representatives, and on Thursday and Saturday nights they drink a couple of shots with friends because they're actually not as sure of themselves as they appear. At first they wield the power; guys fall all over themselves to get their attention. Back on campus these girls may have seemed unapproachable, and now they look like their greatest sex fantasy.

But all of a sudden, around one o'clock in the morning, the power begins to shift to the guys. The girls have had a little too much to drink and are stumbling, and the boys have all the physical power—they are pawing and grabbing, and you know the rest.[1]

And when the girls wake up in the morning, with bursting headaches and sickly self-esteems, their eyes cloud over. They're as confused as ever about what it means to be a woman, to be attractive to men, and what it is they really want. They've handled their God-given beauty like six-year-olds with an automatic weapon and hurt themselves in the end. Where are our freedoms and choices taking us?

Nothing seems to make me more insecure than when I look at myself in the mirror and think I don't look as good as I should. I see a blemish, a new wrinkle, a sunspot, or a little extra tummy when I get out of the shower, and my morning is ruined.

Why?

I'm desperate for beauty.

The dirty little secret is that even though I'm a proper citizen, a liberated woman, a dutiful wife and mother, and a regular churchgoer, I've subconsciously and consciously bought into the millennial message that beauty is power, or, as Naomi Wolf describes in her controversial but eye-opening book, *The Beauty Myth*, a currency like gold.

Media and advertising have successfully done their job by lowering my generation's self-esteem and making us insecure about our bodies like never before. As Maureen Dowd says in her *New York Times Magazine* article, "What's a Modern Girl to Do?," "It's just an aesthetic fact, more and more women embrace Botox and implants and stretch and protrude to extreme proportions to satisfy [society] ... Now that technology is biology, all women can look like inflatable dolls. It's clear that American narcissism has trumped American feminism ... before it was don't be a sex object; now it's be a sex object."[2]

> *"Wearing makeup is an apology for our actual faces."*
>
> —Cynthia Heimel

I try to tell myself, "Get a grip. There are more important things to worry about in life than looks, like my kids' education, struggling neighbors, AIDS, the war in Iraq." And I do get a grip, for about twenty-four hours, until I wake up the next morning with a new pimple on my face.

The crazy part is that even though most of my friends and I look ten times better at our age than our mothers did, I'm forced to continually compare myself to the girls in fashion magazines and the growing number of anorexic-looking celebrities in the media. I ridiculously fret in my thirties about keeping up with today's beauty images even though I'm extremely blessed and have already realized, even surpassed, every dream I have ever had.

So why am I such a sucker for beauty, letting the quest for it produce anxiety in my life? Why does my generation allow fashion and cosmetic advertisers to tell us what is "in" and what is "out" so that we feel compelled to buy something this very minute?[3] Why are we obsessed with the standards of a multimillion-dollar beauty industry that will forever tell

THE TEN BEAUTY COMMANDMENTS OF A MILLENNIAL GIRL

1. *Thou shalt not look a day over twenty-five.*

2. *Thou shalt not wear any size above a six.*

3. *Thou shalt wear sunscreen and drink eight glasses of water a day.*

4. *Thy clothing shalt look like it is from Neiman Marcus— even if thou can only afford to shop at Target and Marshalls.*

5. *Thou shalt never leave the house without lipstick, deodorant, and a credit card.*

6. *Thou shalt not rebuke thy neighbor for using Botox or other injections.*

7. *Thou shalt get a manicure and pedicure every two weeks.*

8. *Thou shalt get a massage and bikini wax once a month.*

9. *Thou shalt only eat protein, fruits, and vegetables.*

10. *Thou shalt not let any diamond grace thy hand if it is less than three carats.*

us we're not beautiful enough? Someone please hit me over the head with a crowbar!

LIFE BEFORE PARIS HILTON

After I graduated from college, I spent several years overseas. As an American, it was like living in a time capsule for nearly a decade. In Paris, the world's fashion capital, I rarely felt insecure about my appearance. I didn't have to. The rules weren't all that complicated. In France, a woman's sense of style is revealed by the care of her skin, a silk scarf strewn around her shoulders, the quality of her shoes and handbag, the aroma of her perfume, and the way she entertains. Women rarely dress seductively or reveal much skin unless they are sunbathing topless on the Riviera. But that's another subject. Most of my French friends didn't wear

46

makeup and would laugh hysterically at America's obsession with inch-long acrylic fingernails and size-E breast implants. They'd rather spend their hard-earned cash on good cheese and wine, a fresh bouquet of exotic flowers, a ski vacation in the Alps, or violin lessons for their kids. These things communicate beauty to them.

Meanwhile, something was changing in American culture, a seismic shift in women's appearance. Think Paris Hilton. Perhaps I felt it more intensely because I moved from the fashion capital to the celebrity-cult capital, Southern California—where, as my cousin Sheila says, "We're so close to Hollywood that everyone wants to be a star."

I noticed a dramatic swing in the United States to more provocative clothing. It was as if Playboy had started new clothing lines at Macy's and Target. Other indigenous trends began popping up everywhere, too—bared bellies, tattoos, body piercings, exposed undergarments, you name it—anything was possible and no longer shocking.

I didn't realize when I left the topless beaches of France that I'd be subjected to so much cleavage back in the United States. What happened? Why was I feeling the lure of such seductive nonsense and superficiality? Had females truly traded in the image of Equal-Rights-and-Equal-Pay Feminism for Lipstick Feminism, which defines self-empowerment with sexual empowerment, girly culture with its penchant for lewd sex appeal?

As Wolf writes in *The Beauty Myth*, "The influence of pornography on women's sexual sense of self has become so complete that it is almost impossible for young women to distinguish the role of pornography in their lives."[4] Pornography's pull is so prevalent that many women anywhere between fourteen to fifty-four are concerned about the size of their breasts. In fact, surveys show that some are so enthralled with bigger busts, and so greatly beholden to Pamela Anderson's measurements as the ideal, that they'd gladly exchange theirs for hers.

"Current ads for Svedka Vodka feature a fembot made of steel, sporting a curvy backside and a come hither posture. 'The future of adult entertainment,' reads the tag line ...What's so unsettling is that the tag line could very well be true," exclaims Kristin Tillotson, columnist for Minneapolis' *Star Tribune*.[5] Today, many of the granddaughters of the women's liberation movement are getting breast implants and Brazilian waxes; their idea of sexual freedom is flashing and making *Girls Gone Wild* videos. Forty years after women picketed for equal rights, female Olympians pose nude in male magazines. Glammed-up strippers are the main characters on MTV and video games. I hardly believe this kind of "female menagerie" was what Susan B. Anthony had in mind.[6]

Ariel Levy, author of *Female Chauvinist Pigs: Women and the Rise of Raunch Culture*, recounts how females acting like males limits their sexual freedom. They are pressured to behave like porn stars, take aerobic pole-dancing classes, and are buying thongs in the millions.[7] Teen girls are learning that being as hot as possible is the ideal, while the rest of us cringe, thinking, *How can so many young females have lost sight of breaking through the glass ceiling for the sexual ceiling?*

THE TYRANNY OF THE SKINNY

According to Wolf, if pornography is one side of the coin, then anorexia is the other. Anorexia affects 2.5 million Americans and has the highest mortality rate of any mental illness, yet Hollywood insists on glamorizing it incessantly on the cover of *People* and other gossip magazines. Who isn't anorexic or anorexic-looking these days? Jessica Simpson, Paris Hilton, the Olsen twins, Lindsay Lohan, Angelina Jolie, and a plethora of other fashion icons. Shows like NBC's *The Biggest Loser* and ABC's *Extreme Makeover* sensationalize radical weight loss, and *America's Next Top Model* pits beautiful bodies against one another. America witnessed *Survivor's* Danni Boatwright's frame shrink down to one hundred pounds when the show ended, and Nicole Richie seems to be competing with Paris Hilton to look skeletally rich and famous.

The title of a *Newsweek* cover article last year on anorexia claimed, "Fighting Anorexia: No One to Blame."[8] However, I question if the growing number of naïve parents and the media's obsession with thinness may be killing our citizens. There must be a link somewhere. Girls don't starve themselves for fun. Whether they realize it or not, they're under societal pressure to be thin. But why do we spend so much time making our lives and those of everyone else miserable?

TAKING BACK GROUND

In the past, women who complained about beauty standards were considered "feminazis." In the arena of culturally imposed female beauty standards, this kind of woman fought for the right to choose what she wanted to look like. She spoke out about the media's promotion of certain beauty ideals for the purpose of making money. Where

Signs of Anorexia

• LOSES WEIGHT DRAMATICALLY

• REFUSES TO EAT CERTAIN FOODS

• OBSESSES OVER BODY WEIGHT

• MAKES EXCUSES TO AVOID EATING

• EXERCISES FANATICALLY

• FREQUENTLY WEIGHS HERSELF

• DENIES BEING HUNGRY

• ACTS MOODY, DEPRESSED, WITHDRAWN[9]

are our fashion feminazis today? Where is the voice crying out in the wilderness, "Why have we traded our sense of equality for sexual enslavement? Why do we feel like we need to wear as little clothing as possible to get a man's attention? Why, in spite of the advancements in young women's education, are we witnessing an increasingly sexualized ideal that the media is forcing girls to live up to?"

I remember a youth pastor telling our church congregation, "We're going to enforce a dress code at the spring retreat because none of your parents will." Everyone laughed nervously, but there was a sense that parents aren't parenting like they should anymore. The media, rather than parents, is setting the dress code.

However, women are beginning to speak out. Though I may not agree with them on every issue, I am indebted to their sagacity when it comes to their fight against ridiculous beauty standards. In *Are Men Necessary?*, Maureen Dowd wrote, "I always assumed that one positive result of the feminist movement would be a more flexible and capacious notion of female beauty, a release from the tyranny of the girdled, primped ideal of the '50s. I was wrong."

Forty years after the dawn of feminism, the ideal of feminist beauty is more rigid and unnatural than ever. When Gloria Steinem wrote "All women are bunnies," she did not mean it as a compliment. "It was a feminist call to arms."[10] Isn't it time we begin building lives for ourselves in the Promised Land instead of Sodom and Gomorrah?

In a culture confused and apprehensive about our female beauty, we need a clear message for young women about what beauty is and what it is not. As Karen Lee-Thorp and Cynthia

Hicks share in their book *Why Beauty Matters*, "When women are anxious about matters of appearance, it doesn't help to tell them, 'Inner beauty is all that matters; how you look doesn't count.'" We need to share constructive ways to challenge the airbrushed perfection of the fashionista world. We need to identify ways that consumerism pressures us to spend money to keep up with the ever-changing standards of beauty. We need to learn how to resist the cosmetic industry's ability to "checkmate" our attempts to feel good about ourselves.

In addition, there is a shortage of good mothering and inter-generational collaboration these days. As Wolf explains, "The links between generations of women need mending ... young women are dangerously unprotected, unguided ... and need role models and mentors."[11] Younger women need to spend more time with older women and see firsthand how true beauty is captured in a winsome smile and in the bright eyes of a woman who loves others and herself.

> *"Overcoming food temptations has replaced sexual temptations as the symbol of female virtue."*
>
> —Jean Kilbourne,
> MEDIA CRITIC

The Church is silent in many respects, seemingly allowing for double standards. We never hear messages about beauty battles on Sunday mornings. In their quest to attract as many youth and singles as possible, many churches entertain well but do little to show how to live holy lives or to plan for their future as spouses and parents. Sociologist Amitai Etzion says, "We must be ready to express our moral sense, raise our voice a decibel or two about what we really believe. In the silence that prevails, it may seem as if we were shouting; actually we were merely speaking up."[12]

The real issue has nothing to do with whether or not women wear makeup—it's seeing ourselves as we truly are. It's having a clear starting point. We are created in the image of God, not Calvin Klein or Ralph Lauren. Genesis 1:27 says, "So God created human beings in his own image, in the image of God he created them; male and female he created them" (TNIV). Every life is sacred, regardless of station or circumstance, skin coloring or physical qualities. Lancôme cosmetics, *InStyle* magazine, or *The Bachelor* television show can't tell us who we are or the value of our appearance.

BREAST IMPLANTS IN THE NUMBER OF FEMALES EIGHTEEN AND YOUNGER HAVE INCREASED 400 PERCENT SINCE 2002.[13]

In her book *Fantasy: An Insatiable Desire for a Satisfying Love,* Betty Blake Churchill writes:

> The truth is we haven't seen or experienced real beauty ... because no one has seen God, no one can begin to imagine the depth and mystery of infinite beauty. Our sense of beauty is just a taste, really, of what is beautiful—God himself. The value of beauty lies in the fact that it is a reflection of him. He created us in his image and as a means of pointing people to himself. The value is short-changed when beauty becomes an end in itself.[14]

LET'S PLAY DEFENSE

So, what is our best line of defense against beauty anxiety and the never-ending message that we need improvement? Should we begin bombing the New York offices of *Glamour* and *People*? Sounds tempting, but it goes against my pacifistic tendencies. Naomi Wolf says, "It's misplaced energy to reform the market, but we can drain the power."

How?

We can learn not to judge too quickly and not to treat people as though we live in a caste system. We must remind ourselves, "Just because a woman looks beautiful doesn't mean she feels it, and she can feel beautiful without looking it in the first glance. Thin women may feel fat, young women will grow old. When one woman looks at another, she cannot possibly know the self-image within that woman."[15] For me, a call to arms means keeping my thought life in check and turning away from those ugly thoughts that creep into my mind when I compare myself to others or when I start to panic that I am not attractive enough. It means walking past the perfectly manicured woman at the M·A·C makeup counter or the highly toned girl at LA Fitness and telling myself, *I am okay where I am. They have some good things in their life, and so do I.*

THE SISTER SIN

On a deeper level, I also need to recognize that my quest for beauty is wrapped up in the need for perfection. Like many women, I'm a perfectionist. I live in a world that is constantly threatening my sense of equilibrium—9/11, the war in Iraq, tsunamis and hurricanes, the growing divorce rate, AIDS, and drug abuse. I desperately need to feel like my piece of the pie—my body, my home, and my neighborhood—is in order and stays beautiful.

Like Eve, I'm disappointed by life outside of the garden, and my sin is the irrational belief that my environment and I must be made perfect. I have a persistent need to accomplish anything I attempt in life without digressions, mistakes, or unattractive qualities. I fear failure and rejection, and my attempt at beauty and perfection are the commodities I can trade for the respect of my peers. I tell myself untruths—that

I will be perceived as a loser if I don't appear to have it all together and stay in step with the culture at large.

This kind of perfectionism and the quest for beauty only lead to more consequences. I will suffer from lower self-esteem, guilt, pessimism, and obsession until I accept that subversive media, advertising, and social systems bent on getting us to spend money will never let us off the hook. They will exist as long as we believe their false and unattainable image of beauty. Technology will give us images of über-thin and über-gorgeous models, and advertisers will always tell us that "retail therapy" is the cure for our depression and unmet desires.

> THE FEDERAL RESERVE BANK PUBLISHED A STUDY IN 2005 THAT SHOWED THAT BEAUTIFUL PEOPLE MAKE MORE MONEY THAN NOT-SO-BEAUTIFUL PEOPLE.[16]

I must remember that my identity is found in Christ, that I'm a child of God (John 1:12), that I've been justified (Rom. 5:1). I'm complete (Col. 2:10) and a citizen of heaven (Phil. 3:20). Today I focus on my character and the gifts God has given me. I remind myself that He richly supplies me with more of Himself, even if my image is decaying (Prov. 31:30).

If you are like many of the college women and young professionals I work with, you need to come to terms with the fact that human life is often marked by failings, weaknesses, deviations, and imperfections. Backsliding in the arena of imposed beauty standards is not the end of the world. You will need to let go of unrealistic, rigid standards that steal your joy and make you feel less human. You will need to avoid women who are competitive and stop listening to criticism about your appearance. You will need to recognize that unrealistic beauty standards weaken women's solidarity, creating fear and jealousy among us. In this sense, we oppress one another as women. We become guilty of creating a class system because we attack one another, even if only in our minds, and judge each other based on the ever-elusive ideals of fashion profiteers.

Working through beauty issues and finding a place where I feel good about my image depends on a change of mindset more than a change of appearance (Ps. 139:14). I'll also be faced with choices. Like so many other choices in an affluent culture, those related to beauty are complicated. Not impossible, not horrible, but complicated.[17] What one woman chooses to do may have an influence on others—breast implants, workouts with a trainer, glycolic facial peels, manicures and pedicures, teeth whitening. If our mindset is positive, we will be free to make the choices that best suit us individually.

Today, when I struggle with my appearance, I try to take a breath and focus on the things that give my life purpose and value. I take time to enjoy the people who love me and believe in me. I put my best energy into the things I know I'm uniquely created for. I try to take care of myself, eat well, take a walk with my four-year-old, call a girlfriend who makes me laugh, get enough sleep, and hope my complexion looks better in the morning. But I also have to admit I'm aging—and there's no Fountain of Youth. I choose to believe that the people around me can value me in spite of my imperfections, wrinkles, thinning hair, and saddlebags. Some days I look better than others. I'm doing the best I can with what I have been given, and in the meantime, I wait for my heavenly body.

NATURAL REMEDIES AND CURES FOR BEAUTY AILMENTS

All sorts of beauty procedures are available—we have to

choose wisely and look for ways to reflect our true identity and priorities in life. So how do we resist the temptations of the beauty industry? How do we make the right choices? Take some comfort in knowing that you are not alone. The quest for beauty goes back thousands of years. Chances are, your ancestors felt some of the same pressures you feel today. If you take the time to connect with some older, wiser women, they'll probably have stories to share and guidance to offer. In the meantime, here's some advice from someone who is a little further down the road than you might be.

• Ask yourself, *Do the things I buy or the changes I make to my body take away my problems or add to them?*

• Use your money wisely. Do not allow the latest trends, which are here today and gone tomorrow, to dictate your spending habits. Don't forget to save for a new car, graduate school, a home, or children.

• Cultivate positive self-esteem through godly character and service to others, not through worldly and ever-changing fashion standards.

• Never use your sexuality as a weapon or a form of currency. Such things degrade God's image and hurt the advancement of true female liberty.

• Believe that your true beauty radiates from within, through your eyes, your voice, and your earnestness, to help make the world a better place.

• Trust that beauty is also expressed through the ancient arts of hospitality, generosity, recreation, and love.

• Deconstruct your beauty myths—figure out what lies to discard and what values to hang on to.

• Read magazines and interpret media programming differently. Be alert to the subtle but toxic ways it affects your self-esteem and love for humanity. Say no to oppressive messages.

Take heart—true beauty awaits you. Here is some additional advice from a female comrade who didn't feel beautiful until she was in her thirties. The transformation didn't just result from a weight-loss program or a makeover. Instead, she experienced an inner revolution that manifested itself in the way she dressed and moved, in the quality of her smile and the light in her eyes. Others started noticing the glowing beauty, too. Lee-Thorp, a graduate from Yale, writes:

"For us, the pursuit of physical beauty [has become] disconnected from any notion that the role of beauty may be to point us to God."

—Lilian Calles Barger,
EVE'S REVENGE

Pride tells us to exploit our beauty to get what we want, or feel ashamed of our ugliness as the proof of our worthlessness. Fear tells us to veil our beauty so we won't draw the envy of other women or lust of men. But when we choose to become aware of and grieve over our pride, shame, and fear, they lose their grip on us. When we allow ourselves to be loved and invest our energy in loving others, we genuinely grow more beautiful.[18]

Chapter 4

DESPERATE
FOR
INTIMACY

*"Women need other women. We wither in isolation; we
blossom with nourishing friendships."*

−BRENDA HUNTER,
PhD, psychologist, and author

When I was seven months pregnant with my first child, I
moved to Paris. I planned to spend the first year focusing on
the baby, learning the language with a private tutor, and then
eventually working part-time with international students.
Meanwhile, my husband immersed himself in an intensive
language program, surrounded all day by interesting people
from all over the world. In hindsight, my move to a new
country as a new mother landed me in a very lonely situation.

I hadn't anticipated how much I'd need the language, family,
a church, parenting classes, play groups, but most of all, deep

friendships with other women. At first the adrenaline of the birth and the miracle of having my own son carried me. Being analytical in nature, I received comfort from reading baby books and establishing a routine for Quinn. Luckily for me, he was an easy and compliant baby! But soon his routine didn't satisfy my longings for authentic and meaningful contact with other adults, particularly women. I was making slow progress in learning the language, which created a curtain between my neighbors and me. In the dead of winter, sometimes I'd go as long as three weeks without a significant conversation with anyone besides my husband. I love him, but I need more than a male perspective. I desperately needed some girlfriends.

I remember calling a French mother, Ann, who spoke English, and asking her if we could get together on a weekly basis. I needed at least that much female contact to keep my head above water. Thankfully, Ann agreed in her French way, "Pourquoi pas?" (Why not?) I didn't feel slighted that she didn't ooze with American charm—I was desperate for someone to hang out with.

This woman was a queen! She began having me over for gourmet lunches on Thursdays and cool dinner parties with other couples over the holidays. More people! Sure, my French was still poor, but I had a blast. I loved watching how Ann and her husband, Didier, worked together as a couple to serve their guests. Didier kept the wine glasses full—two for each person— and cleared the table after each course. Ann always served five to six courses. She flitted back and forth between the kitchen and the dining room, serving up such delicacies as homemade pumpkin soup, salade nicoise, beef burgundy, a platter of five or six different cheeses, dessert, and chocolates served with coffee at midnight. She was the kind of woman I wanted to call a personal friend!

Ann also became a mentor to me in France. She taught me how to fasten my son more securely in his car seat, as well as how to wash salad greens properly and make homemade salad dressings. She took me to her favorite stores, introducing me to fine French perfume and designer silk scarves. She attended my son's baby dedication and told me I spoke French like I had a hairball in my mouth. The French have a particular way of speaking their minds, don't they? I took it with a grain of salt, because Ann was my first friend in France, and I'm forever indebted to her. Funny how good friendships are that way.

THE FORGOTTEN ART OF FRIENDSHIP

"Women need other women," explains Brenda Hunter, PhD, author of *Home by Choice*. "We wither in isolation; we blossom with nourishing friendships. We need our female friends in the good times of life, and we especially need them when we are grappling with the loss of a spouse, parent, or friend."[1] If you're single and long for the intimacy of married life and family, let me warn you: marriage and motherhood can be extremely lonely experiences in our modern world. I love my family and wouldn't trade places with anyone, but it's isolating to try to raise super-children and to compete fiercely in a competitive world. "Conquer, conquer, conquer ... trying to dominate [the world] at every twist and turn" is the way Robert Coles, a child psychiatrist, describes the ways of the millennial family.[2]

It's a full-time job to be a domestic woman these days; there's so much pressure to make sure your kids are perfect. You have to monitor their television and computer time. You have to police their diet and hygiene activity. You have to screen their phone calls, new friends, and even their friends' parents. You have to check their homework. You have to chauffeur them to karate, ballet, Boy Scouts, piano, swim team, youth group, a family therapist, or an ADD specialist. No wonder mothers are so exhausted!

More and more, young women are growing up in homes

with divorced parents, far from grandparents, uncles, aunts, cousins, and childhood friends. They receive the cavalier message that relationships are temporary, potentially hurtful, and untrustworthy. Females learn from their battered parents' marriages how to protect themselves so their lives don't unravel. A young woman who holds on too tightly to the idea of making her home a secure fortress will have no time or energy to develop intimate friendships—the friendships that bring levity to her world and her soul.

The millennial woman is suspicious of other women. She is always running, looking over her shoulder to see how far she can outpace the crowd and keep their influence as far away from her children as possible. I think of the women I would have loved to go deeper with, inside their hearts and souls—but life always seemed to get in the way. They had so much to do, so many activities to juggle. As Judith shares in *Perfect Madness*, these women seem to feel that their life "is a delicate house of cards, held together by the most intricate balancing of all its carefully selected components, and that the slightest shock, the slightest jar to all the perfect orchestration, will bring the whole edifice down."[3]

What a paranoid way to live!

Women who buy into the idea of creating a perfect world, who turn themselves inside out, who fall into bed exhausted every night and have little time for their own authentic adult relationships, suffer the most. They cut away their soul until they believe that they don't need friendships anymore. They think their family completes them. They think their church completes them. Their light slowly dims under a sanctimonious bushel.

Those who manage to find time to step outside the parent pressure cooker tend to have the greater degree of peace.[4] As a Christian, I find that the women who are able to cherish both their children and the people outside their "family castle" have the greatest joy. I learned this firsthand after moving back to the United States with two young children. Life as a mother in America felt like a three-ring circus. I'd never seen so many ambitious women before in my life—women who had "professionalized" motherhood. They were the most educated women in history! Lawyers, accountants, educators, scientists— all giving up powerful careers to spend gobs and gobs of quality time with their kids.

So committed are these women to their children's academic and extracurricular performance, church involvement, workout routines, healthy dietary practices that they have virtually no time for real friends. Sure, they get little fills, like race-car drivers at a pit stop, catching up on the local gossip at Jimmy's baseball practice or Susie's dance lessons—but nothing like the friendships I witnessed in Europe.

Some may chalk it up to "cultural differences," but Europeans—really, most of the world—have us beat in the area of hospitality and entertaining when it comes to cultivating friendships. In Paris, I became accustomed to dinner parties that lasted until midnight, where the kids fell asleep in front of a video or in their parents' arms. I became used to afternoon teatime that began at four and lasted until six. I became familiar with mothers and children congregating at the nearby park, with boxes of cookies in hand, sometimes until nightfall. Sure, there was homework and dinner with dad to think about, but not nearly the crazy schedules many American parents subject themselves to these days. No rushing from one event to the next, gulping down fast food or Starbucks coffee while living in their SUVs as part-time chauffeurs. *Mon Dieu!*

Even French mothers who work full-time seem to effortlessly prepare elaborate meals on Sunday afternoons and still meet friends downtown for coffee and window shopping. Husbands and wives enjoy entertaining together, putting aside money each month for expensive wines and cheeses that they offer in love to their cherished friends. This is how I learned the art of friendship as a young mother.

The difference between Americans and most Europeans is that Americans are much more driven—which is both good and bad. The good is that we are productive and successful as a nation; our kids have high self-esteem and are ambitious and creative. The bad, I fear, is that we are losing the capacity to enjoy genuine human connection. As Christians, we must never lose sight of the greatest commandments—to love God and to love others.

RELOCATING: THE PAIN OF STARTING OVER FROM SCRATCH

If you are like me and many of the women I know, chances are that you've moved recently, are in the process of moving, or will move in the near future. It's simply a fact of life. Countless women go off to college, start careers, marry, and relocate because of jobs, divorces, remarriages, etc. More than 20 percent of the American population—nearly fifty million people—move each year. Many of these feel traumatically uprooted, cut off from a support system. The sensation can leave you feeling like you've had a part of your body amputated.

It's important to understand what you're going through and to know that you're not alone. As Vance Packard shares in his book *A Nation of Strangers*,

> We are seeing a sharp increase of people suffering alienation or just feeling adrift, which is having an impact on emotional and even physical health. We know there is a substantial increase of inhabitants suffering a loss of community, identity, and continuity.

These losses all contribute to a deteriorating sense of well-being, both for the individuals and for society. In all this disruption of familiar patterns, some people respond with a deepened sense of loneliness.[5]

Some of us will feel a greater degree of isolation and loneliness than others. Jill just moved to Seattle from a small community outside of Denver. She's single and working for the first time as an accountant. Her parents are thrilled that she landed such a great job and want to see her succeed. While she earns a good income and is valued by her employer, however, Jill feels insecure and unsure of her future. She misses her friends back home, many of whom are getting engaged or having children. She wishes she had a boyfriend—someone to share her life with.

As the weeks go by and she finds herself spending most weekends at home alone or shopping for work clothes at the local mall, she questions her new life as a "working girl." Sure, she's making good money, driving a new car, and furnishing a new apartment, but she has no one to enjoy it with. Relationships in the workplace haven't gone anywhere and neither have the ones at church. She's not into the club scene or the "Starbucks scene"—hanging out with a book in hand, hoping to meet someone.

By Christmas, Jill's feelings of loneliness are intense, and she dreams of leaving her job and going back home. She feels trapped. There are few women her age at the office, and the young people in her apartment building seem to already have full lives. She puts in her notice on Valentine's Day and calls her parents to tell them she's coming back home. Seattle is too heartless a place to live, she tells them. Her parents are grieved but tell her she's welcome to live with them until she can find employment again.

Jill is so depressed when she returns home that she gives up accounting and gets a retail job at a local department store. Her heart aches from the failure of not living up to her parents' expectations. She lacks direction and wants to feel like a normal person again. She wants to hang out with old friends until she feels confident enough to re-enter the professional life. In hindsight, she should have found a job closer to home in the first place, she tells herself.

The transition from college girl to working girl is not as glamorous as you might think. Like Jill, you might be asking yourself, *Why have I worked so hard in college and in establishing a career, only to feel so alone in the world? Shouldn't a good education and job help you meet quality people and make friends easily? Why is it so hard to meet people who aren't competitive or shallow? Where have all the real people gone?* As my daughter Elena says, "Why can't I have a friend who really cares about me?"

The only place I can take my eight-year-old when she is let down by her friends is to the Lord. I tell her that her heart is so big, no one can ever fill it the way she needs it to be filled. She feels things so deeply that no one can ever feel with her completely. The vacuum inside of her is meant to be filled by love itself. "And so we know and rely on the love God has for us. God is love. Whoever lives in love lives in God, and God in them" (1 John 4:16, TNIV).

So I wipe her tears, stroke her arm, and pray with her: "Lord, fill Elena with Your supernatural love. Help her to find rest in You. Help her to remember there are many people in the world who do care for her and appreciate her even if they aren't always available or notice when she's hurting. Thank You, God, that You always keep Your eye on Elena and can fill her right now. Help her to find her rest in You."

When you question why no one seems to notice you or if you are tired of begging for friendship, go to the One who will truly listen and care for you. Cry out to Him. Tell Him you need His love. And wait to see how He provides you with a friendship you've been dreaming of (1 John 4:7–11).

Amy, who works in the arts and media in Washington, D.C., has this to share about her need for authentic relationships, especially with older women:

> Even as a strong-willed woman who is a follower of Christ, I know deep down that it doesn't end with me. God has been extremely gracious to me beyond the cross. He has allowed me to be in environments where I am constantly challenged both in my heart and intellect with the Gospel. However, no matter how many classes I take and Bible studies I lead, there will always be a need to have someone speaking into my life. Without strong women in my life to look up to, run to, chatter all over, and cry in front of, I'd be lost! When I find that rare woman who doesn't act as though she knows everything, but does, I feel led to seek her out, to soak it all up. It means being bold enough to recognize our need to look to someone else who has walked the path we have but is still willing to go alongside of us as we experience it for the first time.

WOMEN NEED INTIMATE FRIENDSHIPS

Perhaps you are thinking, *I can't really relate; my life feels full of relationships and responsibilities.* Perhaps you could apply the things you learn from this book and help the women in your life who are struggling. Believe me, there's a good chance that someone in the next cubicle at work or the pew next to you on Sundays is dying for a genuine friend. She's looking into your eyes and asking herself if she can trust you with her heart.

As Christians, are we so busy that we are missing the opportunity God has given us to reach out to women who desperately need to experience His love through our lives? Are we so consumed with hyped-up lifestyles and raising our kids like little gods that we don't have margins in our schedules to have coffee with a new neighbor, give them a list of our favorite doctors and hairdressers, or offer to baby-sit so they can enjoy a much-needed evening alone with their spouse? Have we lost sight of the rich Christian traditions to help those who are experiencing traumatic life circumstances, stuck in a painful place, or dealing with the loss of a job, the birth of a child, a divorce, or the death of a parent? Have we so easily forgotten what it feels like to be a stranger and to start over again?

In his book *Living Like Jesus*, author Ronald Sider says that genuine Christians should seek to show the love of heaven by living out Jesus' final words to His disciples. "Love one another. As I have loved you, so you must love one

> ## EMPATHY
> *The ability to imagine yourself in someone else's position. It is the ability to stand in others' shoes, to see with their eyes, and to feel with their hearts. It is something we [can] do spontaneously, an act of instinct rather than the product of deliberation. Empathy isn't sympathy— that is, feeling bad for someone else. It is feeling with someone else, sensing what it would be like to be that person. Empathy is a stunning act of imaginative derring-do, the ultimate virtual reality—climbing into another's mind to experience the world from that person's perspective.[6]*

another. By this everyone will know that you are my disciples, if you love another" (John 13:34–35, TNIV). "God wants [His children] to be a preliminary picture of the kingdom that Christ will bring," Sider writes. We have the glorious privilege of living out that reality in the way we treat people every day.

When you move every couple of years, you're forced to look at yourself and the world around you differently. Sometimes passages of Scripture come to life like never before. In the Gospel of Matthew, Jesus said, "If anyone gives even a cup of cold water to one of these little ones who is known to be my disciple, truly I tell you, that person will certainly be rewarded" (Matt. 10:42, TNIV). This passage reminds me of my most recent move from Southern California to Orlando, Florida. It was a painful move; after so many years as a global nomad, I had grown to call California home. Four months after the move, I became despondent and disillusioned. I felt like no one had room for me in their lives despite my repeated attempts to take the initiative (ask my kids—I am the type of person who will invite complete strangers into our home for afternoon tea). My only contact with other mothers involved carpooling to school or youth group and a brief "Hi, how are you?" in the church parking lot. Depressing!

I missed the network of relationships I had spent nearly five years building back in California. Though they weren't perfect, I had women in my life who remembered my birthday, wanted to get together as married couples for dinner parties, complimented me on a new outfit, celebrated my publishing successes, and swapped baby-sitting.

Then one day, something pleasant happened. I learned that Elena had taken a walk around the corner with some kids and had been invited to play inside the home of a new neighbor. It startled me at first to think Elena was with strangers. But instead of panicking, I put on my flip-flops, headed over to introduce myself, and took a moment to assess the situation.

Ten minutes later, to my surprise, a smiling mother named Jackie greeted me at the door and invited me in for a cup of tea. *Wow!* I thought, *Now this is my kind of neighbor!* Not only did this woman serve me a cup of tea in her fine china, she also offered me some delicious homemade banana bread and took an interest in my life. I couldn't think of any place in the world I would've rather been. She was speaking my "language."

Meanwhile, our daughters forged a fast and furious friendship, which led to carpooling, sleepovers, special birthday outings, Halloween neighborhood potlucks, and an invitation to Jackie's family to visit our church. As Dee Brestin says in her book *The Friendships of Women,* "When [I am with] my female friends I feel my soul is being sunned."

MAKING ROOM IN OUR LIVES FOR OTHER WOMEN

The hardest thing about moving and starting over for me is that I often feel like I have to sell myself or beg people to make room in their lives for me. If we are not busy trying to convince people we are worthy of their time, we are busy trying to figure out who we are in light of a new move. As Judy in Maryland shares, "Every time I move, I have an identity crisis. I question, 'Will people like me?' I wonder what to reveal about myself and what to hide. I'm often guarded, edgy about what I say or don't say. I'm uncomfortable with having to explain myself over and over because people don't know my history."[7]

If you can relate to Judy and feel desperate for intimacy and genuine friendship, you're normal. Millions of people move every year and experience the same feelings. Don't get too down on yourself. Your circumstances are more a reflection of the crazy world we live in than your "attractability" as a friend. These are also the times when we must go to God to fill us with His abiding love. Cry out and tell Him that you are lonely and heartsick. He is the only source of true and eternal friendship.

Remember Ann? One of my all-time favorite experiences with Ann in France was a crazy, out-of-this-world shopping spree nearly a decade ago. I get giddy just thinking about it! It was the kind of shopping extravaganza you see on a show like *Extreme Makeover*. I share this story with you because it represents to me one of those unique opportunities in life that only a friend could offer, something that will be cherished forever. Ann let me into her private French world—a real delight—even though I was a foreigner. I wish every international or immigrant who has to start over in our land could have a friend like I had in Ann.

> "And I pray that you, being rooted and established in love, may have power, together with all the Lord's people, to grasp how wide and long and high and deep is the love of Christ, and to know this love that surpasses knowledge—that you may be filled to the measure of all the fullness of God."
>
> —Ephesians 3:17– 19, TNIV

I had only been in France for a couple of months when Ann called me one day and asked if I wanted to help her spend a big fat $2,000 check she'd just received from her father. Think about what that amount could buy ten years ago! The man was a retired general, or something important, and needed our help to buy a going-away gift for the director of his retirement home. He had collected the money from about forty other residents. The gifts we were to purchase had to be very classy for this bourgeois crowd.

Ann and I checked our calendars. I was still nursing a three-month-old and could only be gone for three hours at a time. Together we drove into the heart of Paris on a Saturday afternoon in her Peugeot and gave ourselves a two-hour time limit. We headed to the nicest and largest department store in Paris, the Galleries Lafayette, a place I'd only heard about but had never ventured into as a new mother on a limited budget.

Ann was amazing, as many French women are. She decided blue was the color and "going on a vacation" was the theme. The clock was ticking! We ran breathlessly from one department to the next, laughing and scheming on what items would meet her grandfather's highest standards of perfection. It didn't matter that we were buying for a stranger. At that moment we were doing as we pleased and dropping cash like rock stars.

Two hours later we had purchased a blue suede weekend luggage set ($750), a dark blue handbag ($450), an attaché case ($350), a shimmering Pierre Cardin silk scarf ($250), and a sophisticated bottle of Boucheron perfume ($200). Wow! We had done it!

Ann took the items home, wrapped them in shiny blue paper, and delivered the gifts to her father the following day. Needless to say, Ann's father and the retirement-home director were exceedingly pleased. I'll never forget the wonderful opportunity Ann gave me in her French world. She could have called someone else to join her, but she had her eye on me, figured me out, and knew I'd probably enjoy it the most. *Merci, ma cherie!*

When we are single and young we naturally make friends and are often open to new friendships. Students, in particular, have an amazing capacity to entertain a lot of people in their lives. But as we age, become busy, worry about finances, and raise kids, we tend to start shutting down relationally. Sure, we care for people all day long, but it doesn't mean we really care about them. We too easily forget how we felt when we were strangers, starting over again.

What kind of a friend do you long for? What kind of a friend do you want to be? Will you be a friend who accepts people just as they are, encourages them, holds them accountable, affirms their good qualities, serves them unabashedly, and prays for them faithfully? Will you share in their celebration and sorrow, birth and death, tears and laughter? Will you put aside worldly standards and accept them unconditionally? Will you allow yourself to enjoy them—quirks, failures, and all? Our love and devotion to each other is the same love and devotion that Christ has for us. Because God freely gives His love to us, we can share it with others.

I want to tell you about my friend Kirsten. She's busy with two little boys, a new puppy, and a very successful businessman husband, but she somehow always has time for me. She gives me hope that there are "real people" out there who love to have fun and still act like a girl. I'm hoping you have a Kirsten in your life, too. If not, start praying for one.

I've known Kirsten since I was ten years old. I was dark like the evening sky, and she radiated the sun's light. We complement each other perfectly, right down to our all-grown-up, five-feet-eleven frames. We were inseparable until high school—that is, until boyfriends came along for her and sports and academics for me. She was the looker of the two of us back then. I'd like to think things have balanced out since then!

She was with me when my mom died of leukemia, and she

sat beside me in the limousine on the way to the cemetery. She let me move into her bedroom when my dad left my brothers and me in her mother's care for months at a time. She bought me my first Bible and showed me how to read it. She begged me to help her with makeup and give her "advice" about boyfriend troubles, making me feel smart and sophisticated. She'll speak to strangers in elevators and sing to Journey in a French pub. She makes me laugh so hard I cry. She's my greatest fan, someone I can be authentic with, who accepts me as I truly am—a control freak who loves the limelight. There were times I took her for granted and even hurt her, but she's remained my faithful and intimate friend—the sister I never had.

Even though my dearest friends[8] live thousands of miles away now, I still hold on to the memories of our time together in my heart, believing in the gift of friendship and the possibility that it can happen again. I need to keep my heart open and my radar on. It may happen at the checkout line at Target, at my preschooler's gymnastics class, or even in the church parking lot. Maybe, just maybe, I'll meet a genuine friend one day soon.

Chapter 5

DESPERATE FOR SOLITUDE

*"Settle yourself in solitude and you will come upon
Him in yourself."*

—TERESA OF AVILA

Have you noticed how hard it is to find peace and quiet
or a moment of solitude? Some unstructured time? Some
kick-back-on-the-couch-with-a-juicy-novel-and-a-bowl-of-
popcorn kind of rest and relaxation?

"Read!" Most of my friends laugh at the thought. "Who
has time for reading anymore?" With three hundred emails to
respond to, babies to nurse, houses to clean, bills to pay, Bible
studies to lead, and careers to pursue, the few who manage
to find time to actually read have to join book clubs to force
themselves to get through at least one book a month.

Many women these days are mercilessly busy. They no

longer know how to give themselves permission to rest or do something for themselves. In our drive for perfection, we're not only working to bring our own lives under absolute control; we're busy shoring up for the rest of the world—wiping down toilets, chauffeuring, loading the dishwasher, checking homework, filling in for a sick Sunday school teacher, and walking the dog at six in the morning because no one else will! Am I describing your world? If not, I will be, in the blink of an eye. A girl becomes a woman. The woman becomes a mother. And the mother has no time for herself.

But it wasn't always this way.

One of the things I treasured about working with university students was their capacity to hang loose, chill, and disengage from the real world to do something meaningful for themselves. When I'd visit these young women in their dorm rooms or college apartments, they'd often have their stash of watercolors, sketching pencils, or journals strewn about their living space. It didn't mean they were taking an art class. These young women intuitively knew how to unwind and get in touch with their existence. They collected music and literature. They took tons of photographs and created digital movies. They baked and experimented with recipes. They made time for museums, film festivals, dance recitals, or friends' theatrical plays. They ordered pizza at midnight, then got up early to see the sunrise before falling back into bed again.

Where is that girl inside of me? I know she's in there somewhere. I want to find her again, and I hope it's not too late. I don't want to be fifty and in the middle of a midlife crisis before I give myself the freedom to enjoy life and make time for myself again. I'm not talking about "rewarding" myself, like splurging on a new handbag, but about getting away by myself. Solitude.

For me, solitude is that undistracted time when I can close

the door and hear my thoughts and the thoughts of God. It's disengaging from the world and letting my mind drift to the magical land of possibilities, the life I truly want to live. I could be reading or taking a walk or soaking in a bathtub, but I am alone, and I feel the love and power of God envelope me. I dream about possibilities and hear God whisper ideas I've never considered before. I hear His corrections, His plea to slow down and love the people around me better. The sensation infuses me with life, hope, and a sense of expectancy—like a schoolgirl in love again. When was the last time you experienced it? I know, you can't remember.

WHY ARE WE SO TOUGH ON OURSELVES?

For many, parents may be a culprit. Quiet moments were rarely valued or modeled in our homes. Few of us saw our parents live out their private lives in a way that communicated it was okay to make time for ourselves, to practice the spiritual discipline of solitude. They bought into the baby-boomer lie that more is better. They wanted us to be independent and competent, to make our own money and control our own destiny. They didn't teach us how to grow a garden, how to kick back on the weekends with a warm blanket and good book or play board games as a family by the fire. We were always in the car, going to some event, doing some activity, or sitting in front of the television. We heard the emphatic message that "girls can do anything"—and that meant doing, not being. So we became demanding and failed to learn one of the greatest lessons in life—that sometimes, doing nothing is the most powerful experience of all.

In order to achieve the level of perfection we believed we had to attain, we had to be productive. Club soccer, youth group, piano lessons, Girl Scouts, homework, volunteering—you name it, we've done it. As Warner describes in *Perfect*

Madness, "There can be no distracting personal or avocation detours—[we] must be unrelenting in the pursuit of goals. No one can do anything if it doesn't involve doing everything and doing it all at an incredibly high level of performance. Men have always known this; they don't even try."[1]

It's the last line that really gets me: "Men have always known this; they don't even try." Why do modern women have such a hard time letting go and enjoying their personal lives a little more? Why is it that men can take thirty minutes out of their day to go outside and hit a bucket of golf balls or fish in a nearby pond—and we can't? Why do men give themselves permission to stop by the local pub after work to grab a drink with their buddies or take a Sunday afternoon nap—and we don't? Because we let them?

No.

Because they let themselves. We should, too!

Men don't walk around with a "save the world, or else" complex the way many women do. They've still hung on to their inner boy. Men naturally turn on the football game, break out a deck of cards, or play chess after dinner while women start loading the dishwasher. Why is that? Is it as one friend says: "That's just what moms do"? Possibly, but I think it's more complicated than that. More often than not, I think we don't give ourselves permission to read a magazine or take a walk because we feel the need to always fix things and don't give the men in our lives a chance to help us out.

I've got to stop telling myself, "My house needs to look perfect, spotless, like the pages of a decorating magazine." Because when I do, I beat myself up for missing the mark of perfection, and I'm left feeling too tired to address my greatest needs. Too tired to read. Too tired to soak in the tub. Too tired to play with my kids. Too tired to love my husband. Too tired to write. Too tired to pray. Something's got to change.

A DAY IN THE LIFE OF AN EXHAUSTED MOTHER

6:30 A.M.   Puppy begins to whine—needs to go potty and eat breakfast

7:00 A.M.   Preschooler begins to whine—needs to go potty and eat breakfast

7:30 A.M.   Wake up school-aged children, who whine because they don't want to get out of bed

8:00 A.M.   Make lunches; unload dishwasher; make beds; take a shower

8:30 A.M.   Give children a ride to school

9:00 A.M.   Run to Target for much-needed supplies: toilet paper, cereal, dog food, milk

9:45 A.M.   Painter arrives to paint living room

10:00 A.M.   Preschooler begs for a morning snack and a play date; walk puppy; do laundry

11:00 A.M.   Painter needs more paint; run to the paint store

12:00 P.M.   Pick up neighbor's child to play with preschooler; make them lunch; fold laundry

1:00 P.M.   Make coffee; try to write for two hours (with many preschooler interruptions)

3:00 P.M.	Pick up school-aged children; walk puppy
4:00 P.M.	Prepare afternoon snack and check children's homework; arrange for more playtime with neighbors
4:45 P.M.	Attend son's basketball game
6:00 P.M.	Make a quick dinner; eat together; ask children about their day
7:00 P.M.	Clean up; spend time with family; help children with spelling words
8:00 P.M.	Get kids ready for bed; read a book and pray with them; set out morning clothes; walk puppy
8:30 P.M.	Spend a few minutes with husband to catch up on news at work and review the calendar
9:00 P. M.	Brush teeth; put on sweats; fall into bed, exhausted.

A couple of times each year my husband finds sanctuary at a local spiritual retreat center. He fasts, plays his guitar, takes a walk, and talks to God. He comes away from that time renewed and believing that he's heard from God. Sometimes it's a simple message such as "love people more," and other times it's more dramatic and may require a job change or relocation. He does this because it brings both God and him much joy to commune intimately, without the distractions of the world. Though I don't like being left at home alone with the kids, I relish my husband's arrival after a spiritual retreat. He's glowing, mellow, attentive, and more gentle. He's the man I married again.

We've been married for more than a decade, and I have yet to enjoy a personal retreat. Sure, I've been on spiritual retreats— but with fifty other women. I have a good time, but I wouldn't use the word *refreshed* to describe how I feel when I return home to three wide-eyed children. Frankly, I am wiped out from so much interaction with so many people and so much information. I have just spent forty-eight hours with a group of women ... how can that be refreshing?

What I need are some serious moments of solitude. Like most of my peers who are "over-controlling mothers," I don't give myself enough permission to leave my family for more than a few hours at a time. This is something my generation feels extremely guilty about because we've been taught to "overprotect." Young mothers need to realize it's okay to leave the kids with dad for the weekend and get the rest they need.

> *"Let [her] who cannot be alone beware of community ... and let [her] who is not in community beware of being alone ... Each by itself has profound pitfalls and perils. One who wants fellowship without solitude plunges into the void of words and feelings, and one who seeks solitude without fellowship perishes in the abyss of vanity, self-infatuation, and despair."*
>
> —Dietrich Bonhoeffer,
> *LIFE TOGETHER*

CULTIVATING PEACE THROUGH MOMENTS OF SOLITUDE

The letters originally penned by François de Salignac de La

Mothe Fénelon, the Archbishop of Cambri, France, during the
seventeenth century, speak of the great need we have to let go
of our insecure and selfish need to strive incessantly. Fénelon
was the spiritual adviser for a small community of believers
in the Court of Louis XIV who sought to live a life of true
spirituality amidst a society that was decadently immoral.

Fénelon wrote to his pupils, "Learn to cultivate peace.
And you can do this by learning to turn a deaf ear to your
own ambitious thoughts. Or haven't you learned yet that the
strivings of the human minds not only impair the health of
your body, but also bring dryness to the soul. You can actually
consume yourself in too much striving ... Your peace and inner
sweetness can be destroyed by a restless mind."[2]

Have you lost your inner sweetness? I don't mean to sound
facetious. I know millennial girls are characterized by anything
but sweetness. But how about an ability to remain tender,
open, and hopeful under the strain of modern life? Or have
you, like so many others, become increasingly cynical, overly
analytical, and suspicious toward people and life in general?
Isn't it time to turn the *Titanic* of anxiety and stress around?
Where do we find refreshment for our souls in a desert with
no streams? How do we resurrect our inner girl and begin
cultivating our imagination? How do we find that quiet space
in our lives again to reflect, create, pray, and dream?

Another culprit for me is the huge invasion of technology
in my life. The computer easily zaps fifteen to twenty hours
of my time each week. I get my news online, do research for
my writing projects, check my kids' basketball and homework
schedules, check out the prices of the real-estate market, and
... you know the rest. Add to that millions of women who
chat, shop, listen to music, and watch short films online. Like
characters from *Star Trek: Enterprise*, we spend more time in
front of a monitor than participating in real life.

For others, it's the battle of television that robs them of their much-needed quiet time and leaves them numb and unable to think beyond everyday responsibilities—it becomes survival on a shallow and linear plane. We watch television so we don't have to hear ourselves worry, obsess, or think about what we still don't have.

Consumerism steals many precious hours of our personal time, too. I am not a big shopper, but I do have a family to care for. This involves grocery shopping and purchasing clothes, beauty products, school supplies, cleaning supplies, and the latest gadget advertisers tell me I need. We spend our resources and time on redecorating, collecting more throw pillows, wall hangings, candles, and hand towels. We have become so hooked on creating the "perfect" home that we forget what it means to build our "home lives." Moms take their kids to the mall when they are depressed or angry instead of showing them how to work through their feelings or wait for self-gratification. Shopping has become a form of therapy.

So how do we cultivate peace and learn to turn a deaf ear to our toxic, ambitious thoughts? How do we avoid running ourselves into the ground? How do we make time for some solitude in our loud and busy lives?

First, we must see solitude or silence as a positive experience, not a negative one. Some women may actually be afraid of time alone. As Richard Foster says in *Celebration of Discipline*, "The fear of being left alone petrifies people ... our fear of being alone drives us to noise and crowds." We have, in many ways, become dependent on noise and activity to make us feel alive, purposeful. We become anxious when we have nothing to do. Unfortunately, we miss the opportunity that solitude offers us for much-needed rest and reflection—the kind of stillness that enriches our world and the quality of our relationships. For example, I feel a greater sense of compassion and desire to be attentive to others after I have spent some time alone. As Thomas Merton says, "It is in deep solitude that I find the gentleness with which I can truly love [others]. The more solitary I am, the more affection I have for them. It is pure affection and filled with reverence for the solitude of others."[3]

Elaine's a young mother of four living in rural Kansas. Even though she's busy caring for her family, she makes time at the beginning of the day for solitude. She describes her need for peace and quiet:

> Solitude is as important to me as water is to life. When I forget to water my plants, leaves start turning brown, and eventually the whole plant wilts. If I neglect solitude for very long, I experience discontentment, anxiety, and even depression. As a young adult, I learned the necessity of taking time to be alone. It has not always been easy to keep up the practice! Having had four children at home on a full-time basis for twelve years greatly interfered with my need for some peace and quiet. I now know I need to find creative ways to take a break from the demands of motherhood: swapping kids with friends, requiring kids who have outgrown naps to play quietly in their rooms for part of the afternoon, asking my husband to give me an evening off each week, and going away on an annual personal retreat. I have to continually remind myself to ignore the shouts of the world that cry, "You're only valuable when you are busy!" and to heed my heavenly Father, who whispers, "Be still, and know that I am God."

Solitude requires giving yourself permission to be alone once in a while. This will be harder for some than for others. One of the reasons we resist solitude is that it make us feel useless or empty. We are used to controlling the world around us, and we get anxious when we are not moving all the time. We need to learn how to disengage from the nonstop demands of work, relationships, and parenting, and allow others to step in for a few moments to give us a break. It may also require organizing our time better so we have time in our schedules to take a breather and re-energize. When we are quiet, we have the opportunity to trust God more.

I often find that when I take twenty minutes out of my day to lie down, read, or pray, new and life-giving thoughts fill my mind. Some of my greatest ideas for writing, media, and ministry projects have come to me during five-minute showers. As a mother of young children, sometimes a shower is the only "alone time" I get during the day. But when I can be alone, I find I hear from God more clearly. I turn over in my mind new ways to approach a problem or obstacle. I sense my shortcomings and remember to apologize to my loved ones. I am more tender

> *"Without silence there in no solitude."*
>
> —Richard Foster,
> *CELEBRATION OF DISCIPLINE*

and encouraging toward them. I also experience the magic of greater creative ability—new story lines, new plots, new twists, new publishing angles, or new marketing strategies. And that's just in the realm of writing. *Wow!* I think. *Imagine when I will have several hours to myself someday when the kids are all in school!*

THE SPIRIT-FILLED LIFE

Perhaps you are new to the idea of cultivating solitude in your life but sense that you need it as desperately as I do. Let me share the secret to finding those pockets of silence in your life and then walking in newfound strength and joy, the inward journey that unleashes God's presence and power in your life, the connection between being quiet and listening to God. It can open you up to the Spirit-filled life.

What is the Spirit-filled life? It's not a new fad or a self-help concept. Thousands of years of history speak of His work in mankind. The Holy Spirit is not a vague ethereal shadow or an impersonal force. It's equal in every way to the oneness of the Father and the Son, sharing their divine attributes. Jesus said, "I have come that [you] might have life, and have it to the full" (John 10:10, TNIV). He desires to awaken and harness us with His power and His Spirit living in us.

By faith we can be filled with the Spirit, experience intimacy with God, and enjoy His attributes manifested in our life: peace, love, courage, and hope. In John 14:26 and 16:13, He promises that the Holy Spirit will guide us into truth. When we claim His power and walk in His Spirit, we unlock the door to victory and joy.[4] The Holy Spirit equips every willing Christian for fruitful service. Paul wrote in Ephesians 3:16–17, "I pray that out of his glorious riches he may strengthen you with power through his Spirit in your inner being, so that Christ may dwell in your hearts through faith" (TNIV).

If we genuinely yield ourselves to God's will and sincerely surrender ourselves to Him by faith, He will fill us (1 John 5:14–15). We may not have an emotional response, but rather a calm assurance. In time we will experience a greater faith, boldness, liberty, and power to live the life we were meant to live (Gal. 5:22–23).

Why did Jesus come into the world? To seek and save the lost (Luke 19:10). We are lost as long as we attempt to live our lives on our own. With the increasing pressures of a rapidly changing society, we strive for perfection and control that only

God can offer. But He's not so concerned with the kind of perfection and control we think we want this side of heaven. He wants us to know Him, walk with Him, and allow Him to be a part of our lives. And it's in those times of solitude and silence that we can begin to understand His mysteries and will for our lives.

Will you make time for Him? Will you make time for yourself? Will you surrender yourself and be filled with His Spirit? Will you allow Him to reveal His marvelous plans for your life and show you how to enrich your relationships with your loves ones?

We can have confidence in the authority of the Scripture and the testimony of millions of Christians throughout history and around the world today that God will fill us just as He did His early disciples (Acts 1:8). An exciting journey awaits you. Solitude. It's as simple as closing your door or taking a walk outdoors. A mystical land where you can hear the whispers of God, who offers healing and the joy of knowing you were marvelously created for His great story. To be cast for the greatest role of your life, you will need to put your faith in the trustworthiness of the Director. As I walk by faith, I can know, even in times of uncertainty, that I am in good hands. He has proven Himself time and time again and taken me to higher and higher mountaintops. All He asks is for us to "be still, and know that I am God" (Ps. 46:10, TNIV).

My friend Louise had an awakening to the power of solitude in her life. As a result, she has begun to mentor other women and encourage them to be still before God. Here's what she has to say about her need for some peace and quiet:

For me, solitude is time alone, without noise, without distractions—it has become an essential part of my life. This is the place where I get in touch with what is real and true and where I connect with who I really am in my deepest self. It is also where I connect with God within. I need quiet places in my life to hear God's voice and to be reminded that I am loved and that God is with me, here and now. It is an ongoing communion of my soul with God that I take from my quiet place into my hectic and often noisy life. God fills me with love and a knowledge of His presence. This enables me to better respond to the people and situations of my day. When I don't have time for solitude, I tend to react rather than respond. Solitude puts me in a place where I can listen to others with love.

Chapter 6

DESPERATE FOR FINANCIAL SECURITY

"For the love of money is a root of all kinds of evil."

−1 TIMOTHY 6:10, TNIV

Josh and Lauren met during their junior year at the University of Michigan through the Greek system and became fast friends. Josh liked Lauren's sharp mind, sophisticated sense of style, and fearless ambition. Lauren liked Josh's down-home values, the way he made her laugh, and how he brought out the young girl in her again. Lauren's mom was an Army bride from Japan, and her dad died when she was in elementary school. She was a driven student and meticulously plotted out her career path. She had a high need to secure her own happiness.

After graduating from college, Josh and Lauren found themselves working in the same city two thousand miles from home and resumed their amicable relationship. One thing led to another, and a couple of lonely months later they decided to move in together. Sex didn't drive the decision so much as a desire for companionship during the hard transition from student life to adult life. They enjoyed entertaining together on the weekends and sharing war stories from work—he in advertising and she in banking—and slowly, their love for one another grew. Both were very talented, but Lauren had a

> 77 PERCENT OF
> AMERICANS SAY
> RELATIONSHIPS
> [NOT MONEY] ARE
> THE SOURCE OF
> HAPPINESS. [1]

particular spark in her that spoke of greatness. She was going places, and her future success seemed limitless.

Fast-forward seven years. After two homes, two dogs, several exotic vacations, and a five-star wedding, Lauren and Josh called it quits. They parted on friendly terms, supposedly. Lauren said she wanted to focus more on her graduate studies, and Josh said he didn't feel like he loved Lauren anymore. But everyone else got the sense that Lauren outgrew the relationship. Josh and Lauren didn't want the same things anymore. Her passion for success, and the monetary security and pleasures that come with it, outpaced her commitment to her husband. She wanted more—a lot more than Josh could ever offer her. So she was going to go after it. And she was convinced the best way was to do it alone. Though there were other factors involved, Lauren was very influenced by a brand of feminism that says, "If you are not happy in a marriage, get out."

THE MANY FACES OF FINANCIAL FREEDOM

We may go to the altar and vow to stick together "for better or worse," but the reality for many couples is that when it comes to money, it'd better not be for worse. Thanks to the magical world of media and advertising, many people under the age of thirty-five grew up with a sense of entitlement and privilege. An increasing number of couples between the ages of twenty-seven and thirty-seven are ending their marriages in divorce. We believe a comfortable life is possible, attainable. We believe in ourselves, and we set goals for success. Even though we hear tales of our parents having lived in tiny apartments and struggling to make ends meet, we want the big house with a gourmet kitchen and the shiny SUV parked in the garage by the time junior arrives.

As you can imagine, this puts a lot of pressure on young couples to achieve their dreams at lightning speed. Sooner or later, even happy marriages can rapidly disintegrate when a young couple comes under financial duress. The numbers don't add up, and dreams suddenly feel out of reach for a few years, maybe longer. Then the wife may start to panic and operate defensively.

She may say that marriage requires sacrifice, but when the freedom and power she associates with money in her marriage begin to dissolve, so do the trust and loyalty she once pledged to her partner. *I can do better than this*, she might tell herself. Money problems show her core convictions. Her feminist indoctrination has taught her to mistrust men as potential slackers when it comes to providing—so she had better take the reins.

John Gottman shares this about the young couples he counsels in Seattle: "Whether their bank account is teeming or they're just scrimping by, many couples confront significant money conflicts. Often such disputes are evidence of a perpetual issue, since money is symbolic of many emotional needs—such as security and power—and goes to the core of our individual value system."[2]

Before you react too harshly or kill a potentially lifelong relationship, I hope you will consider the danger of loving money a little too much. Research has proven that once your basic needs are met, more money does little to raise your level of happiness.[3] If you are looking for a more satisfying life, invest in relationships. Those with the greatest levels of happiness and fewest signs of depression have strong ties to family and friends and a commitment to spending time with them.[4]

More and more marriages end today because the wife wants out. I look at my peers under the age of thirty-five who have divorced, many with no kids or young children, and often the reason for divorce is another man or financial incompatibility. The woman may want more than her husband can provide her—more time, more affection, more status, and often, more money.

Many of my peers have been bred to see themselves as winners, and when they don't feel like winners financially, they start to get a little skittish about commitment—and then their need for security wins out. For many, financial security implies the ability to pursue their dreams. And they don't want anyone to hold them back. Some work aggressively to build a career, while others simply put more pressure on their spouse to make more "for the family."

There seems to be a certain level of income that every couple believes they can achieve and depend on. The numbers differ for every couple. But when they fall below that amount, they may become prey to marital disaster. Certainly husbands have their own share of struggles, but the stress some wives feel from discovering that their financial security is not as reliable as they had hoped may cause them to question other "givens," like the marriage commitment. Some women will simply walk out or disengage from their husbands emotionally when the money starts to run out. They may not turn to divorce, but they will look for new ways to meet their needs. Some stop trusting in their husbands—and, ultimately, God.

Singles deal with these issues as well. I hear about it from my single brother and his compatriots. Money is a bigger issue in dating than perhaps it's ever been. In cities like Los Angeles, New York, Seattle, and Washington, D.C., it's hard to get a second date unless you can prove your net worth or own a home. Young men who pursue their dreams in teaching, the arts, music, or the literary world—in other words, less lucrative fields—have the hardest time finding women to commit.

Bill is a professional guitarist and full-time student at the University of Florida. After graduating high school, he spent seven years touring with successful bands all over the country. The pay wasn't great, but it was the chance of a lifetime. Bill started dating Lydia eight months ago. Their relationship quickly took off, and before long, they decided to purchase a small, fixer-upper home and move in together. Bill began college, teaching guitar lessons on the side, and he quickly became strapped for cash. After paying tuition and his portion of the mortgage, there wasn't much left to enjoy his relationship with Lydia. No more money for romantic dates or gifts. No more money for new furnishings and the promised remodeling projects. Ten weeks after moving into their new home, Lydia decided to end the relationship and moved out. Bill was in shock. He thought his intentions had been clear— he had been thinking long-term, marriage. But Lydia had met a successful and wealthy businessman at work she'd rather be with. Bill felt devastated that he'd not only lost his girlfriend but would also have to sell the home.

Of course, there's a lesson here about "not putting the cart before the horse," or something like that, but Bill was hurt badly when Lydia chose a man with more money. He felt directionless and insecure about dating again. Perhaps it would be best to put off serious dating until he finished his studies in a couple of years. "Are women really that heartless these days?" he questions.

On a side note, while many young couples are choosing to live together before marriage, most cultures and faiths around the world look down on it. Christians are encouraged to keep the marriage bed holy; sexual intimacy is to be shared between a man and wife alone. This is not only for their pleasure, but also for protection from potential heartbreak and spiritual demise. Even though our culture may be fickle, scriptural mandates regarding sexual purity are timeless for believers of Christ.

Bill's story is not all that unique—just ask the men in your life how greatly money affects the dating scene. They feel the double standards perhaps as intensely as you do in other areas. There are a lot of Bills out there who are brokenhearted because their girlfriends are ditching them for men who hold the pot at the end of the rainbow—big fat pots of diamonds, cars, and cash.

> *"No one can serve two masters. Either you will hate the one and love the other, or you will be devoted to one and despise the other. You cannot serve both God and Money."*
>
> —Matthew 6:24, TNIV

You see, smart, sophisticated girls often picture themselves with lawyers, doctors, and real-estate brokers who sell million-dollar homes. There's always hope that some rich guy is around the corner. Call this selfish greed, but young women these days want their independence just as badly as they want to kick back and be mothers someday who drive luxury vehicles, carry designer handbags, have a cleaning lady, and enjoy their morning macchiato from Starbucks. Blame Hollywood or our baby-boomer parents who didn't teach us "family values," but women are more desperate and insecure about money today, and it's wreaking havoc in our lives. We are like broken cisterns, never completely full or satisfied.

Back when I was dating, money wasn't really an issue for me. I was poor, so I didn't care how much the guys I dated made either. We were young and all starting out together. The future was wide open with possibilities, but money was never a driver in my decision-making process. I loved people and adventure more than the idea of a big salary. It wasn't so difficult in the early years of marriage either, especially since we were overseas. I didn't mind living simply on a fixed budget. Most of my married neighbors owned just one car—and tiny cars at that. They had few appliances. A dryer was a luxury. And they lived in apartments no larger than eight hundred square feet. No one had the space to collect the things we do in the States. Good, hard-earned money was used on relationships, children's extracurricular activities, entertaining, and vacations. My children were still small at that time, so my concerns didn't go much beyond groceries, diapers, decent winter coats, shoes, and an occasional getaway to a nearby bed and breakfast. Life was so much simpler back then.

For me, the need for greater financial freedom came after we moved back home to the Untied States and the kids entered school. My view of money changed dramatically as I started looking around at what everyone else had and began to internalize the same frantic obsession. All of a sudden, I began to think that my kids needed the best that modern life could offer: swim team and piano lessons, braces and horseback-riding camp. Something shifted in my relationship with both my husband and my checkbook.

I needed more money, and I needed it badly. I panicked

and worried that I might let my kids down if I couldn't help
them keep up with their peers and express their individual
dreams. I also felt pressure from some friends and relatives to
have a higher standard of living—after all, I wasn't in school
or living overseas anymore. They wanted more for me, and
frankly, I wanted more, too. Not in the way of material things,
like fancy cars and jewelry or designer clothes and furnishings,
but the freedom to be able to be creative and raise my kids
in a way that I thought was right. For me that meant an
excellent education and a commitment to athletics and the arts.
The list became longer every year as the kids got older. But
the numbers didn't add up, and I ended up questioning my
husband's ability to provide. I got frustrated and angry. I was
desperate for financial security.

Then one day the stadium lights went on. God spoke to
my heart. I realized the shortsightedness and foolishness of
my dilemma. My problem was that I wanted my husband to
meet needs he was never designed to meet. He couldn't read
my mind or anticipate how motherhood would create in me
a desire to provide extravagantly for my children. He thought
I had married him because I loved him, but suddenly I was
changing the rules, asking for so much more. My expectations
were shifting and deepening beyond levels he was prepared to
meet. I wanted him to be someone he wasn't, and this brought
a lot of heartache into our relationship. He wasn't sure how
much to accommodate me and had no guarantee it would
really make me any happier.

Looking back, I had wrongfully put my trust in my husband
to meet my financial needs rather than God. I had forgotten the
lessons I had learned as a college student and a single woman.
Matthew 6:25–33 had become my life verse at college when I
began trusting God for the finances to travel and go on short-
term mission projects. "Do not worry about your life, what

you will eat or drink; or about your body, what you will wear
... For the pagans run after all these things, and your heavenly
Father knows that you need them. But seek first his kingdom
and his righteousness, and all these things will be given to
you as well. Therefore do not worry about tomorrow, for
tomorrow will worry about itself. Each day has enough trouble
of its own" (TNIV). I needed to think like that again.

KNOW YOURSELF

I am moved to greater levels of faith regarding my financial
insecurities when I put my needs and wants back in God's
hand, where they belong. When I look to other people to solve
problems for me, I am less grateful and rarely satisfied. But
when I see God move, direct, and provide, I am always amazed
by His wonderful provisions. I feel that He hears me and sees
me. I remain humble and tender
to the people around me.

Perhaps you are thinking this
sounds like "pie in the sky"
if you're in a tough financial
situation. I don't mean to diminish
the fact that some young women
are in difficult marriages. Perhaps
they chose rashly or did not
anticipate, in the long term, the
kind of person they married. Some
of us didn't properly calculate how
marriage would either enhance
our life or drive us crazy, or were
unable to prepare for unforeseen events that made our financial
situation more difficult. Perhaps we married men with little
ambition or men who want to control and monitor every detail
of our existence. But are men really the problem? Have they

> WHERE YOU LIVE,
> HOW MUCH MONEY
> YOU MAKE, YOUR
> JOB TITLE, AND
> EVEN YOUR HEALTH
> HAVE SURPRISINGLY
> SMALL EFFECTS ON
> YOUR SATISFACTION
> WITH LIFE. THE
> BIGGEST FACTOR
> APPEARS TO BE
> STRONG PERSONAL
> RELATIONSHIPS.[5]

truly let us down financially? Or are we looking at our money anxieties from the wrong angle?

Sadly, a great number of couples are not adequately prepared for the reality and demands of married life. Men typically don't have the same material needs as women. This can cause a lot of friction if you want new living room furniture and a larger clothing allowance when he wants a new stereo or ski equipment. Or if he operates from an abundance mindset

> 81 PERCENT OF PEOPLE WHO MAKE LESS THAN $50,000 A YEAR IN INCOME ARE HAPPY WITH THEIR LIVES.[6]

while you operate from a scarcity mindset. Different values about money can crush the intimacy and security so many couples long for when they join together in matrimony.

In many marriages I've witnessed, it's typically the wife who pushes for the bigger house and the expensive remodeling projects. Mike and Shani spent two years remodeling their new home. Fifty thousand dollars later, Shani filed for divorce. The demands of the projects and the lack of control she felt drove her over the edge. She seethed with anger that she couldn't get everything she wanted and that her husband couldn't understand her expectations. The house was sold six months later, and the material girl moved to a resort community to "start her life over."

Maybe it's time to go back and address the financial expectations in your relationship. Maybe you need to see a pastor or counselor to help you talk things out and trust God more with your money issues. So many of us are confused about the purpose of marriage and the holy covenant God intended it to be. Some of us want marriage to provide the financial security it was never meant to provide. Ultimately, we are communicating that we love and need money more than relationships.

I don't want you to feel guilty if you are struggling with money issues right now. I want to help you look at your insecurities about money from a new angle. If you are anxious or stressed about finances, then take some of the things in this book and try to apply them to your situation. Talk to your family and friends, and figure out what's right for you. Most of all, take your anxiety to God and let Him help you move forward with grace and dignity.

Here's some advice that worked for me. Whether you're contemplating marriage or considering divorce, I'd like to encourage you to take a good hard look at how money and material security play into your decision-making process and the quality of your relationships. If you're looking for someone to take care of you, to belly up to the bank and make your dreams come true, then you're in for some real disappointment. No relationship—I don't care how rich your Prince Charming is— can ever fully meet your needs. Sooner or later your man will resent you, or some desperate desire you have will be out of his reach—and you'll find yourself at square one again, alone.

Before you move forward in a committed relationship, take some time to deconstruct your view of money and your dependence on certain levels of income. What things are essential to you, and what things border on greed and personal insecurities? Ask yourself where you place your value and where you can find the greatest measure of peace. In material things? Education? Status? Relationships? Then step back, take a deep breath, and consider God's perspective. Consider the warning Paul gave to Timothy about money:

> Godliness with contentment is great gain. For we
> brought nothing into the world, and we can take
> nothing out of it. But if we have food and clothing, we
> will be content with that. Those who want to get rich
> fall into temptation and a trap and into many foolish

and harmful desires that plunge people into ruin and destruction. For the love of money is a root of all kinds of evil. Some people, eager for money, have wandered from the faith and pierced themselves with many griefs. (1 Timothy 6:6–10, TNIV)

Paul's message is just as relevant for us today—perhaps even more so, because the temptations are endlessly greater. As educated women evolve and become more liberated, I find myself asking, *Shouldn't we also become more attuned to the shallowness of material wealth and worldly status? Haven't those caused enough problems in the world? Don't they represent so much of what we should be leaving behind?*

If you are experiencing tension and anger in your relationships or marriage due to finances, ask yourself whom you are blaming and how you may need to look at your situation differently. Does God want to provide for you in new ways that you haven't considered before? If you are married, does He want you to take some financial responsibility in your marriage instead of badgering your husband? Or cut back on unneeded expenses? You have options.

Many couples get into trouble because they don't plan for their financial future. In his book *The Seven Principles for Making Marriage Work*, John Gottman shares this with young couples:

> Imagine your life in five, ten, twenty, or thirty years from now. What would be the ideal circumstance? Think of things you want and the kind of life you would ideally like to lead. Also think through the kinds of financial disasters you would most want to avoid ... list your long-term financial goals, taking into account

what you most desire and fear ... share your list with
each other. Look for similarities in your long-term
goals ... come up with a long-range financial plan that
will help you both meet your goals. Be sure to re-visit
the plan every so often to make sure you're still in
agreement.

WHAT DOES YOUR IDEAL LIFE LOOK LIKE FINANCIALLY?

• What are your dreams for the next five years, ten years, and
beyond?

• What kind of a home do you want?

• What kind of a mortgage are you comfortable with?

• How do you want to educate your children?

• How much do you need for personal grooming, fitness, or
entertainment?

• What kind of budget would you like for clothing and
furnishings?

• How much do you want to spend on birthdays and
Christmas?

• What kinds of vacations do you wish to take?

• How much do you need for emergencies like car or house
repairs?

• Do you expect to acquire lawn service, a cleaning lady, or babysitters?

• How much would you like to have in savings?

• How much do you need for retirement?

• How much do you want to tithe?

• What things do you and your spouse agree or disagree on financially?

• Do you need to separate some of your money into different accounts?

• What are some creative ways to earn money for the extras?

• What things can you let go of or wait for until the money comes in?

Women who are strong-willed and independent tend to run ahead of their husbands in the area of finances. But they are also susceptible to making rash decisions without a good frame of reference and the wisdom of others to guide them. They may be suspicious that their husbands don't really have their best interest in mind, but my experience in counseling young couples has shown me that most husbands really do want to make their wives happy—even if they do not share the same time frame or sense of urgency.

My advice to young married women is to give your husband the benefit of the doubt. Express your greatest needs, and ask him to help you plan for financial security and to fulfill some of your dreams. Keep a tender and open heart. Together, plan for the future you want, but don't let your quest for perfection get you in over your head financially.

If you value something that he doesn't, don't harass him about it. Instead, go to God and ask Him to help you find a creative way to make things happen. There's nothing unscriptural about that. He desires the kind of intimacy with you that a child has with his or her parents. "Which of you, if your son asks for bread, will give him a stone? Or if he asks for a fish, will give him a snake? If you, then, though you are evil, know how to give good gifts to your children, how much more will your Father in heaven give good gifts to those who ask him!" (Matt. 7:9–11, TNIV).

For me, it was a private education for my kids in Southern California. I was tired

> *"For compromise to work, you can't have a closed mind to your spouse's opinions and desires. You don't have to agree with everything your spouse says or believes, but you do have to be honestly open to considering his position."*
>
> —John M. Gottman,
> THE SEVEN PRINCIPLES FOR MAKING MARRIAGE WORK

of homeschooling, exhausted, and ready for a change. But I wasn't completely prepared to enroll my kids in pubic school. I figured we'd make the leap in a couple of years. My husband and I looked at our finances and found that private school was too much of a stretch. At that, I started praying, asking God for a way to generate $500 a month for a particular Christian school I had my eye on. I prayed and prayed. Six months later, I was offered my first writing contract (it didn't just fall out of the sky—I had to show some initiative) and received the exact funds I needed to enroll my two children in Stoneybrooke Christian School for two years! Instead of putting undue pressure on my husband to come up with the money, I looked for creative ways to fulfill some of my own dreams. Maybe your story is different. Maybe your needs seem greater, but I know from experience that we have a loving and resourceful God who hears our cries and wants to help us in personal ways.

Financial anxiety and stress are normal for women our age. We are bombarded incessantly by media, as well as well-meaning family and friends, with the message that it's incredibly important to satisfy all of our material needs today. Here is some advice: blow it off. With a grateful and prayerful attitude, do what's right for you and your loved ones. We need to learn to stop looking over our neighbors' fences and coveting their possessions. The way people spend their money is a personal matter. No one can dictate to us what is right or wrong, unless it is against the law. With the same amount of money, one couple may decide to eat out three times a week and spend extravagantly on vacations, while another couple may purchase expensive furnishings or send their kids to private school. Each individual or couple will choose differently. Who are we to judge?

Rather than poisoning yourself and your relationships over money, work to diffuse financial tensions and plan for the future you dream of. Always keep the matter in prayer and attempt to live with an eternal perspective. That means remembering where your true eternal home is. Take heart in the promises of God's Word. "Do not love the world or anything in the world. If you love the world, love for the Father is not in you. For everything in the world—the cravings of sinful people, the lust of their eyes and their boasting about what they have and do—comes not from the Father but from the world. The world and its desires pass away, but whoever does the will of God lives forever" (1 John 2:15–17, TNIV).

THE CHRISTIAN AND STEWARDSHIP

Reviewing the way God feels about money when I begin to panic about finances helps me gain perspective. God owns everything, so my role is to be a good steward of what He chooses to entrust me with. He is the one who gives and takes away. Sure, my part is to be responsible, keep a budget, and invest wisely, but ultimately, He provides for me. Furthermore, He wants me to express my faith in Him by giving to others in need and to the work of the Church. This obedient giving is also called tithing. As I surrender my needs and wealth, focusing on His kingdom, I actively trust that He wants to provide for me. I am His daughter, and He wants the best for me.

Here are some Scriptures to reflect on as you begin trusting God for your financial concerns, keeping in mind that you are a citizen of heaven. Find the ones that bring you comfort. Then take some time to reflect on particular financial concerns and give them to the Lord in prayer. Your future is secure when you put your trust in Him.

LUKE 12:15 "Then he said to them, 'Watch out! Be on your guard against all kinds of greed; life does not consist in an abundance of possessions.'"

HEBREWS 7:2 "And Abraham gave him a tenth of everything."

2 TIMOTHY 1:7 "For the Spirit God gave us does not make us timid, but gives us power, love and self-discipline."

2 TIMOTHY 3:2 "People will be lovers of themselves, lovers of money, boastful, proud, abusive, disobedient to their parents, ungrateful, unholy, without love, unforgiving, slanderous, without self-control, brutal, not lovers of the good."

HEBREWS 13:5 "Keep your lives free from the love of money and be content with what you have, because God has said, 'Never will I leave you; never will I forsake you.'"

2 CORINTHIANS 9:6-9 "Remember this: Whoever sows sparingly will also reap sparingly, and whoever sows generously will also reap generously. Each of you should give what you have decided in your heart to give, not reluctantly or under compulsion, for God loves a cheerful giver. And God is able to bless you abundantly, so that in all things at all times, having all that you need, you will abound in every good work. As it is written: 'They have scattered abroad their gifts to the poor; their righteousness endures forever.'"

LUKE 16:13 "No one can serve two masters. Either you will hate the one and love the other, or you will be devoted to the one and despise the other. You cannot serve both God and Money."

PHILIPPIANS 3:20 "But our citizenship is in heaven. And we eagerly await a Savior from there, the Lord Jesus Christ."

ROMANS 8:28 "And we know that in all things God works for the good of those who love him, who have been called according to his purpose."

Chapter 7

DESPERATE
FOR A
LEGACY

*"God knows the feelings of discouragement, inadequacy,
and failure which conscientious parents feel. But it was
His idea to make them parents and to give them [their]
particular set of children."*

ELISABETH ELLIOT,
The Shaping of a Christian Family

Whether you're single or married, it's likely that if you're
reading this book, sooner or later you'll be a mother. You'll
either have children of your own, adopt, or become the
surrogate mother of a special child brought into your life
through relatives or a friend. Almost every woman dreams of
passing on a part of herself and knowing she can affect another
life for good. For some, motherhood is a chance to recreate the
magical childhood she didn't have, even to re-parent herself.
Others long for children who will fill their lives with color

and laughter, hugs and kisses, and the hope of a brighter future. Most of all, we have an intense desire to improve on what our parents handed down to us, for good or bad, and give our children a better legacy.

My generation seems to have taken parenting to the level of a competitive sport. With more than one million children homeschooled and millions more under the instruction of professional tutors, the future seems limitless in what a mother can offer her child. "If there's a will, there's a way," the saying goes, and today's mothers are capable of raising some amazing individuals—future Olympians and Rhodes Scholars, the next Monets and Mozarts. More and more women are taking their hard-earned education and career training and putting them to "work" in their children's lives like never before. It is no longer necessary to leave the home to feel "fulfilled"—we can do it through our children.

Just as astonishingly, our lives as mothers seem to be riddled with more fear and anxiety than the generations before us. We're smart but scared spitless. We live in a highly competitive world that tells us we had better micromanage every detail of our kids' lives, lest they become losers. Motherhood is quickly turning into what feels like a neurotic obsession. I know, I'm one of those control-freak moms who can't fully enjoy motherhood because I'm desperate to know my kids will turn out okay. Like the growing number of anorexics who learn how to become anorexic from one another, we mothers internalize each other's obsessions (whether it's food, education, sports, or appearance) and try to outdo each other as if our child will get the biggest piece of the pie. But motherhood has not always been this way. Someone please stop the madness!

HOW DID WE GET HERE?

The ascetic form of parenting we take for granted today

began to take root in the 1920s with the scientific method and with fathers becoming the main wage-earners in offices and factories. Women began to have more time at home with their children, rather than working in the fields or as hired help. To occupy their time and energy, mothers were encouraged to more vigilantly monitor their babies' sleep, eating patterns, and daytime activities. They were encouraged to purchase safer highchairs and playpens, to begin singing and reading and increasingly accommodating their lives to those of their children.

Most mothers still had plenty of other responsibilities and relationships to attend to in their communities, however. Several hours of the day were taken up by cleaning and mending and the preparation of home-cooked meals. Children were encouraged to play outdoors, ride their bikes, take long walks, and entertain themselves until the dinner bell rang. Social life revolved around the church and family gatherings. Mothers also had the support of older female relatives or older children to help with the little ones.

As generations became more affluent and couples chose to have smaller families, parenting, as Judith Warner writes in *Perfect Madness*, was taken to a fever pitch. It was no longer good enough to be a good mother, but to be a *What to Expect When You're Expecting* kind of mother. Advertisers and profiteering "parenting experts" ramped up their efforts to convince mothers of better ways to raise their children instead of following the age-old practices of generations before them. There was no limit to the things these "experts" told us our children needed in order to be safe, smart, healthy, and successful. Being a good mom now means buying expensive car seats and baby carriers, educational DVDs and music CDs, luxury strollers and baby cribs, orthodontic pacifiers and corrective shoes, and thousands of other incredibly necessary

gadgets and items at Babies "R" Us. We are told to let our
babies sleep in our beds, nurse them twelve hours a day,
feed them puréed carrots, and carry them on our bodies like
mother kangaroos. We've ended up becoming not only the
most highly educated generation of mothers, but also the
most sacrificial, while the rest of the world, concerned by the
number of divorces and burned-out women, cries, "Chill out!"

The level of anxiety and fear I felt as a parent mushroomed
once I returned to the Untied States. At that time, I had
a six-year-old and a three-year-old, and shortly afterward
became pregnant with my third child—just on the heels of
the Columbine incident and then 9/11. I remember feeling
very afraid to let my children play at neighbors' homes, let
alone outside. I became suspicious of other people's lifestyles,
the amount of television they allowed their kids to watch, and
the things they might expose my kids to. I homeschooled my
children in an attempt to keep them pure from the world's
contamination, stroking both their need for security and my
own.

There were certainly benefits to our homeschooling
experience: the forging of lifelong friendships with other
homeschooled children, the freedom for my kids to learn
at their own pace and explore the world outside of the
"classroom," flexible hours, and more time as a family. The
skills my children learned then have paid off tenfold now that
they are enrolled in a public school, where they are getting
excellent grades and are respected by their peers and teachers.
But part of me regrets the massive amount of time I spent
worrying and the fear that played so much into the way I
educated my kids. I felt an immense burden to protect them
from the world at large, as if evil villains lurked behind every
unseen corner. And I am left asking myself—and maybe you
are, too—if this kind of parenting is really what God intended
for His children.

History will show we lived in an incredibly violent age, one marked by 9/11, the war on terror, and natural disasters like Hurricane Katrina. My heart aches for the thousands of people who've sacrificed their lives for our nation or were the victims of random acts of nature. But few of us truly fall victim to such horrors, and we rarely come into contact with the real victims of crime: the truly abused, poor, and hurting. These images are projected into our home at our own free will. So why is it that the evil we see through the media's lenses—but don't experience firsthand—has such a powerful effect on our parenting style?

Meredith homeschools three children, ages eight, six, and four. Even though she's only in her thirties, she struggles with chronic pain and migraines related to a bout with cancer she had as a teenager. Irritable and tired, she often raises her voice at her kids. But she insists on homeschooling them, like many of her peers, because she's convinced no one can educate them as well as she can.

Myrna Blyth, the editor of *Ladies' Home Journal* from 1981 to 2000, describes in her tell-all book, *Spin Sisters*, how media sells fear to women in America. "*Good Morning America, 20/20, The Today Show, Dateline NBC,* and other shows want you to feel afraid, worried that the next victim might be you or your child. When it comes to selling fear, television and women's magazines live by one rule: there's no such thing as overkill. There's always asbestos in our schools buildings, secondhand smoke, holes in the ozone, high-tension power lines, cell phones that cause brain cancer, and lead poisoning peeling off our walls." And that's not it, Blyth says. The food police warn that "popcorn, margarine, red meat, Chinese, Italian, French, and Mexican food, along with McDonald's, contribute to heart disease." Almost everything—

hot dogs, sodas, peanut butter, caffeine, bottled water, potato chips, tight bras, and cell phones—supposedly cause cancer. Fanned by the media, our fears grow at exponential levels. We begin to believe our children are in the crossfire of real danger every waking moment of their lives. Today's anxiety is then bolstered by a belief that if something goes wrong, if our kids are kidnapped or don't make the soccer team, somehow it's our fault. We failed them and society in general. So we micromanage our family to ward off the contagious evils of the world, hoping our children won't end up as—God forbid—losers. We wake every morning telling ourselves, "If we give them just the right combination of winner-producing things—the right swimming and ballet lessons and learning-to-read books and building toys—we can inoculate them against failure," Warner explains.

Compound this line of reasoning with the fact that many of our parents divorced or abandoned us on one level or another, and it's doubtless that anxiety has always been a part of our existence. We have an intense need to control every detail of our lives because we've always had to. As if we're the lone sheriff of our fortress. Psychologist Janna Malamud Smith shares that for women

> *Melissa spends four to six hours a day chauffeuring her three children, ages ten, eight, and seven, to private school and their extracurricular events. Next year, her children's tuition will reach $25,000. That doesn't include the "extras" she will have to pay for: books, uniforms, school supplies, shoes, birthday parties, piano lessons, and sports. She says she's happy because the kids are happy—and for her, this is the definition of motherhood.*

who lose family or strong family ties to divorce or death, "there's an enlarged sense of vulnerability, personal and social, by becoming a mother—and accepting the intimate mission of keeping dependent beings alive."[1] We therefore obsess, control, and micromanage our children's lives, telling ourselves that if we can get the "formula" just right, we can put a force field around them and keep them out of harm's way. But what is the end goal, really? Has God truly called us to raise little superstars and brainiacs? Does He want us living with so much fear and stress and treating our children like little idols?

Why is is that even though we live in the safest time in history, we live in so much fear? We have vaccines, extraordinary technology, high safety and health standards. School violence, drugs, teenage pregnancy, and abortion are all down—yet we are still terrified because we hear about them so incessantly in the media.

Political scientist Aaron Wildavsky said, "How extraordinary! The richest, longest-lived, best-protected, most resourceful civilization with the highest degree of insight into its own technology is on its way to becoming the most frightened."[2] Sounds like we need to step back and take a long, hard look at ever-growing insecurities. Are they really founded on hard facts or marketing ploys of media moguls? Why do we spend so many countless hours fretting and thinking of the worst possible scenarios? When will we give ourselves permission to enjoy our children instead of plotting their success stories? To stop feeling like we are not okay, when we really are? In fact, we are doing a pretty fantastic job of raising amazing children.

PROFESSIONALIZING MOTHERHOOD

Thirsty for new friendship, with hot cups of tea in our hands, Chloe, Karen, Jennifer, Kim, and I sat around my kitchen table one afternoon. Our preschoolers toddled nearby, playing dress-up, asking for more Cheerios and their sippy cups. As we shared our backgrounds, I was startled to learn that we all came from broken families. Was the phenomenon really so pervasive? Our stories were different but the outcomes much the same. Chloe's father died from a sudden heart attack when she was nine, and she was raised by a single mother. Karen's parents split when she was three, and her mother remarried another man with children when she was nine. Both Jennifer's and Kim's parents divorced after they graduated from high school. And I lost my mother to cancer when I was fourteen and have seen my dad remarry twice since then.

We were all overachieving, college-educated women with international work experience who wanted so much to do the right thing. Somehow we pushed past the pain of how our parents let us down and made significant lives for ourselves. We were also lucky enough to marry, own homes, and have a couple of kids to adore—any woman's dream. Right?

After we said our goodbyes, I turned over in my mind how many other women I had met over the years like Chloe, Karen, Jennifer, and Kim. We are a generation of former latchkey kids (children who come home to an empty house because both parents are working or are absent) who've professionalized motherhood in a desperate plea to somehow make things right again and to validate our own female identity.

We cross the line when motherhood becomes a religion. We cross the line when we become little gods trying to orchestrate every detail of our children's lives, believing that if they aren't perfectly safe or healthy or well-educated, we are somehow to blame. We cross the line when we beat ourselves up because we don't feel like getting on the floor and reading one more book to our kids, when we don't feel like spending every afternoon and weekend in the car chauffeuring them to their activities, when we don't feel like taking them to the mall one more time to buy another outfit for a music or dance recital. We cross the line when we get so anxious and cranky that all our attempts at hyped-up mothering drive a wedge in our marriages and screw up our family because we have allowed the kids to become the center of our universe. Meanwhile, society tells us we are saints and presses us to work harder, run faster, and not give up lest the whole world fall apart.

Susan was so petrified by the terror of 9/11 that she contemplated moving to Montana from her Southern California home. She wanted to protect her kids from any potential bombings and thought Montana might be a safer place to live.

Traditionalists will tell you that motherhood is the antidote against a dangerous and corrupt world. Some mothers believe if they work part-time or make time for themselves outside of the home, they are sacrificing their children's best interest. They tell themselves that they must be home and engaged in some meaningful activity with their children at all times. They feel incredibly guilty at the thought of spending a weekend away with their husband or cultivating another interest, unless it's something "spiritual." They tell themselves motherhood is a season and that they can get their lives back when they are fifty. Get their lives back? Why do we feel we have to give up our lives in the first place? Don't our children need to see their mothers enjoying parenting and their own adult interests simultaneously? Isn't there enough time in the day to love our kids and love ourselves? Aren't our husbands modern enough to help out domestically and give us "permission" to feel like a woman again? I have an inkling that if we loosened our claws a little and stopped trying to be Supermom all the time, many of our husbands would indeed roll up their sleeves and get more involved. Why not give it a try?

Isn't it about time we stopped listening to the spin of rage and fear we hear from feminists and traditionalists and take stock of how much we've accomplished for our kids, how far we've come since our parents' generation? Instead of worrying and fretting all the time, how about looking at our situation from a different set of lenses—one of hopefulness? The book of Proverbs has some great things to say about hope and parenting. The wealth of instruction for parents is summed up in Proverbs 22:6, "Start children off on the way they should go, and even when they are old they will not turn from it" (TNIV). There's simple logic to parenting. God's Word reminds us that if we stick to the basics of raising kids with good character, a reverence for God and people, and a general ability to care for their own bodies and possessions (including their grades, hobbies, and personal living space), they will turn out okay.

As the superintendent of Stoneybrooke Christian School in Mission Viejo, California, once told me, "Kids basically turn out like their parents. If you're godly, hard-working, conscientious, and love and serve people, so will your kids. They see what you do, and they'll want to do the same." *Wow!* I thought, *Could it really be that simple? If I just keep doing what I know is right in my heart and stay close to the Lord, then my kids could actually turn out all right? How freeing!*

After twelve years of parenting three children, I'm finally coming to terms with the superintendent's words and believing her advice. I also see the examples of the grown children of some of my colleagues and neighbors, and marvel at what incredible citizens they've become. For me, I needed to witness it firsthand. Kids I knew when they were five and six are now going off to college with academic and athletic scholarships. They are studying abroad in Italy and Japan. They are starting their own companies and making their own films. They are going on one-year missions trips and helping with relief work in Asia. Some are even getting married in their young twenties and starting their own families. What more could any parent dream of?

Christine survives on three to four hours of sleep a night. Her son, Jeffrey, whom she affectionately refers to as her "little bird," nurses every two hours and finally konks out around two in the morning. Christine also struggles with depression, low self-esteem, and a lack of romantic feelings for her husband. Who wouldn't, with a baby at her breast all day?

If you hope to start a family someday, you'll want a little insight from someone who's been in your shoes. Chances are good that you are isolated or live hundreds of miles away from your relatives or a good support system. Like many young couples, you are probably starting a new career or beginning your life from scratch. Yes, you could easily purchase all the latest baby books and gadgets, but you need a little direction so you can know what the essentials are. Here are some ideas that have worked for our family and helped me to raise children I am proud to call my own:

MAKE GOD A PRIORITY. Pray together, teach them Bible stories, and attend church regularly from the time they are infants. Cultivate a Christian worldview, to love God and to love their neighbor.

SPEND TIME TOGETHER AS A FAMILY. Go for walks, read, play board games, talk to each other, eat dinner at the kitchen table, wrestle, sing, dance—make home a fun place to bond.

ENTERTAIN. Show them the value of other people and relationships. Make your guests feel special. Serve them with love and teach your kids how to do the same. This is how even little kids learn their "pleases" and "thank yous," politeness, and human kindness.

DON'T DUMB DOWN THEIR EDUCATION. Speak to your children from the time they are toddlers about things that interest you, like art, history, geography, architecture, cooking, other cultures, and languages. Visit historical sites and museums. Teach them how to enjoy an afternoon tea (or hot chocolate) and spend time with adults. Give them a taste for the finer things in life, and they will quickly learn to enjoy them.

TEACH THEM THEIR BOUNDARIES. Explain modesty and the need to protect their bodies and respect those of other people. Play down the seductiveness in media and pop culture. Teach them to learn self-control with their eating habits. Help them to respect the environment and other people's property.

ALLOW LITTLE OR NO TELEVISION. Limit television to educational programming or shows that won't undermine your family's moral and spiritual convictions. DVDs are a good way to keep your kids free from the most toxic programming and advertising.

READ TO YOUR KIDS. This will help develop their vocabulary, imagination, and self-control. They will learn how to occupy and entertain themselves through books rather than always going to the television or computer.

DON'T HYPER-MANAGE YOUR KIDS' SCHEDULES AND FILL UP ALL OF THEIR FREE TIME. Kids need time to daydream, journal, draw, play outside, climb trees, fish, sleep in, ride their bikes, and just be kids. The busier they are, the fewer opportunities they have to learn to live life and deepen relationships. They may even become more task-oriented and more anxiety-ridden than we already are.

DON'T COMPARE YOUR KIDS TO OTHERS. Even though it's an incredibly human tendency, do not allow your pride to make these comparisons. Raise your kids with joy, knowing that they are ultimately God's to guide and direct as they approach adulthood.

"Blessed are those who find wisdom, those who gain understanding, for she is more profitable than silver and yields better returns than gold" (Prov. 3:13–14, TNIV). Too often, we invest a great amount of money and time in sports, hobbies, and expensive educational options. These are not bad in and of themselves, but we need to ask ourselves if they are truly preparing our children for the everyday challenges of adulthood. Are we equipping them to care for themselves and others? Are they learning the life skills that will help them to one day get along with their employers and colleagues, neighbors, and future families? Or are they learning that the world revolves around them and that their needs must be satisfied this instant? Are we teaching them that good character and a good work ethic will carry them further than worldly status and materialism? By training our children to be wise, responsible, godly, and loving adults, we are giving them a precious legacy. More than that, we are giving them a future with happy marriages, children, friendships, careers, and a fruitful life in community.

When I pray for my children, I ask God for the essentials. I pray they will remain close to Him, that they will be healthy and safe, and that they will shine His light in every situation. I also pray for big things. I ask that they will go even further than me in impacting the world for good, that they will enjoy happy and healthy marriages and a godly home life. I don't pray that they'll go to an Ivy League college, make lots of money, or live in a big fancy home. I don't pray that they will homeschool their children or become missionaries. I am learning to trust that they will make good choices as we focus together on obeying and listening to God. I also have confidence that as I expose them to a variety of quality life experiences and people, those choices will come naturally to them. I am eager for them to take the lessons they've learned from me and improve on them. Sir Isaac Newton once said, "If I have seen a little further, it's by standing on the shoulders of giants." I pray that by standing on my shoulders, my children will be raised up a little higher and see a little further.

Chapter 8

DESPERATE FOR THE SUPERNATURAL

"God had my attention—my strategy to run my own life was not working."

—NANCY WILSON,
In Pursuit of the Ideal

Ellen grew up in a traditional, working-class family outside of Philadelphia. Her parents were in their forties when she was born and did their best to raise a young female in a rapidly changing society. Even though they never went to college, they encouraged Ellen to get a good education and begin her career as soon as possible. Ellen's zeal for life and love for people helped her succeed at her studies and land a good position as a physical therapist at a children's hospital. As the only child of an older couple, Ellen longed to marry and have her own family someday—maybe even a house with some land, a dog, and three or four kids.

The dating scene proved to be discouraging after she began working full-time. Guys in their twenties seemed more interested in hooking up than in entertaining a committed relationship. Ellen tried to remain patient. She focused on building her career. One day she met an older man at a local eatery. Ben admitted to being twice divorced but hadn't given up his hope of finding lasting and permanent love someday. Ellen listened attentively to Ben's life stories, touched by the comfortable and casual manner in which he spoke to her and attracted to his mature good looks and self-confidence. She was impressed by his description of his growing construction business and his love for the outdoors. Her heart went out to him as he described his attempts at two failed marriages. Both times the women walked out on him to "find themselves," he explained disappointedly. Ellen thought to herself, *Find themselves? What more could a woman want than to be with a man like Ben? He's kind, funny, polite, successful, and good-looking.* It wasn't long before she let Ben know of her interest, and soon, they began a relationship.

Three months later, Ellen found herself pregnant with Ben's child. She was overjoyed. She wanted the baby, and she wanted Ben. Next came marriage and life as a newly married couple. She moved into Ben's two-story home on a couple of acres of land with a rambunctious beagle and a butterfly garden. Life couldn't get any better. Ben carried on with his work and hobbies, and Ellen prepared for the next chapter of her life story. In no time at all she was nicely tucked in with a new baby. It seemed like her dreams had come true. Then, reality hit.

As the adrenaline of the first few months of motherhood wore off and her lifestyle changed, Ellen began to suffer postpartum depression. Ben worked long hours and often grabbed a few drinks with his buddies after work, like in the old days. On weekends, he did a lot of household projects or worked overtime to make a little extra money. He was still affectionate when he came home, but the demands of work usually made him too tired to engage in deep conversation or plan ahead for romance like he did when they first started dating. The honeymoon phase was clearly over.

Meanwhile, Ellen began to feel desperately lonely at home and insecure about her future. Her parents and college friends lived an hour away. Frequently on the verge of tears, she felt like her dreams were caving in. She was unsure about her new identity and scared she'd never find the level of happiness she longed for. Would she be a good mother? Had she acted rashly by marrying Ben so quickly? Did she really love him anymore?

Without the power of alcohol and romance to kindle their relationship, their age difference began to show more, too. Ben became irritable with her bouts of depression. At times, he accused her of being like his other wives— never completely satisfied and constantly looking over her shoulder. Ellen felt confused and scared. Was Ben right? Was she just as heartless as the women who left him before? She wanted to do the right thing, but the feelings weren't there. She sank deeper and deeper into depression. Even though she didn't come from a particularly religious family, she began to secretly pray and cry out to God. She was desperate to know that He saw her and cared about her situation.

"As we make choices, we need to realize that even little ones repeated day in and day out lead us along certain paths, determining the course of our lives and defining the kind of people we will be."

—Poppy Smith, *WISDOM FOR TODAY'S WOMAN*

THE SEARCH FOR MEANING

More and more young women are searching for spiritual meaning in their lives. They are looking for stories, experiences, and relationships that challenge them, surprise them, transform them, and evoke a sense of awe and transcendence in their lives. They want to see the world through the spiritual lenses of beauty, freedom, love, joy, and hope. They want to be inspired in a way that provokes spiritual awakening and a deeper appreciation for life.

With films like *The Passion of the Christ* and *The Exorcism of Emily Rose* on the scene these days, young people are showing a hunger to understand spiritual experiences and to know they are part of a greater story. They are curious to learn if life is lived not only on a material plane but a spiritual one. If God exists, does He see them and care about them?

German filmmaker Philip Gröning's 2005 film, *Into Great Silence,* is a documentary that follows the everyday activities of monks in Europe for six months. "The result, which is just shy of three hours, should be mind-crushingly boring, but it's getting rave reviews. In Germany, it's playing to packed theaters," *Newsweek* reported.[1] There are less than three minutes of dialogue in the whole film, but the chance to witness the sights and sounds of monastic life is appealing: the chants, prayers, lighting of candles, tolling bells, and intimate images of lives devoted to God. Germany is one of the most unchurched and secular nations of the world, yet the turnout at Gröning's film shows that people, even those who are sophisticated and agnostic, long for a radiant encounter with the spiritual realm in their daily activities.

Young women are searching for spiritual answers; they want to know that their lives matter somehow. Relationships will fail us; they cannot satisfy our deepest longings. But we want to know that on a spiritual level God knows us, allows us to be real with Him, and is not afraid of who we really are. In our heart of hearts we know that "superficiality is a curse of our age"[2] and that we must break through the barriers that keep us feeling marginalized, disconnected, undervalued, and unloved. We need to give expression to our hearts' cry for meaning, purpose, authentic love, and spirituality with the people around us and with our Creator.

I come from a multicultural background, with a Muslim, Iranian father and a Christian, American mother. From my earliest years, I lived both in the United States and in Iran, following my father, who was a liaison for an airline. He helped manufacture and purchase planes for the Shah of Iran.

Iran was a modern monarchy before it was overturned by the fundamentalist Islamic clergy who rule today. Similar to scenes from the movie *Catch Me if You Can*, my family lived an exciting, international lifestyle during the Shah's reign—attending private schools and living in rich American compounds in Tehran in the 1970s. At that time, Iran and America were on good terms. Women there dressed like those in the West and had many of the same rights. But things changed radically when the Shah lost touch with his people and the clerics took the spiritual and moral reins of the country.

In 1976 my blond, blue-eyed mother began to sense the stirrings of anti-American sentiment after an American general who lived in our compound was assassinated on his way to work one morning. Several vehicles filled with men and machine guns circled our American neighbor's car and then sprayed him down with the artillery of a small army. At that time, many Iranians were not happy with American policy in the Middle East and the Shah's ties to America's political administration. This was the beginning of the revolt that took Iran back to the dark ages of black-veiled women and bearded, angry men.

The idea of raising her daughter in the Middle East began to frighten my mother. She saw the way Middle Eastern men studied her budding adolescent girl and wanted to ensure that my siblings and I had the greatest advantages and liberties. She wanted to leave Iran immediately and return to the United States. My father agreed to allow my mother to move back and enroll their three kids in school while he remained in Iran for his work. We ended up moving to Bellevue, Washington, just on the heels of the Iranian Revolution and the hostage crisis that began in 1979.

> *"Whom have I in heaven but you? And earth has nothing I desire besides you ... but God is the strength of my heart and my portion forever."*
>
> —Psalm 73:25–26, **TNIV**

For me, it was the absolute worst time to re-enter American life as an Iranian-American youth. I quickly felt the backlash of the hostage crisis from my junior-high classmates and teachers. I had always seen myself as an American, but people started to focus on my younger brothers and me as terrorists. Kids teased us, pushed us, and talked about taking us hostage. I felt a deep sense of guilt and shame about my Iranian ethnicity. And, as if things could not get worse for a girl already grappling with identity issues, my mother suddenly passed away from leukemia when I was fourteen.

At that time in my life, I thought there was nothing worse in the world than to be a motherless Iranian-American teenager. I incessantly compared myself to my classmates, telling myself I was in the worst possible situation. I felt like I was on the lowest rung of society. I wanted so much to fit in, to feel accepted, to be part of the crowd. I needed to know my mixed identity somehow made sense in the grand scheme of things.

But God had His gaze fixed on me. It was during those difficult years, feeling estrangement amid cultural and familial crisis, that an American neighbor named Pam took my brothers and me under her wing and led us to a personal faith in Christ. She became our surrogate mother, arranging our carpools for school and for sports. She bought us clothes for school dances, included us in family holiday celebrations, and finally let us move in with her and her family while my dad traveled back to Iran to salvage his assets and remarry an Iranian woman. A young mother of three children, Pam insisted that we also attend church with her family each week for spiritual and moral direction. We had little parental supervision in our lives at that time. It was at Pam's church that I began to see my need to develop a personal relationship with God. I remember praying one night, "Okay, God, if this is what it takes ... I want You to be a part of my life." He must have heard my prayer, because from that time I sensed His presence in my life more fully and desired to live for Him more intentionally.

At this same church a few years later, I met students who attended Campus Crusade for Christ while I was a student at the University of Washington. Not long after, I joined a freshman Bible study and became interested in international missions. Just as importantly, I began to blossom and feel comfortable in my own skin among my new Christian friends who seemed to appreciate my unique and multicultural background.

Later, I worked with university students in Europe and the Middle East. Surrounded by 100,000 international students, I grew tremendously working among people from so many different parts of the world. I met people with similar stories who had survived wars, revolutions, and politically and economically difficult situations.

In the grand scheme of things, my cultural identity makes a

lot of sense to me today. My international heritage was not a coincidence. I see how, as a child of multicultural parents, I can relate comfortably to people from diverse ethnic backgrounds. I can empathize with their life experiences, suffering, and challenges. Most of all, I value my life story and see God's fingerprints in the fine print.

Amelie, a student in Paris, is from a war-torn region of western Africa. I met her at a student gathering we hosted each week. She was lonely and struggling financially to get by in a sophisticated and expensive city like Paris. But she was desperate to make a life for herself, rather than return to the fighting back home. She needed God to provide friends who could look past her ethnicity and love her as a human being. She found it challenging that some Europeans didn't accept and trust her because of the color of her skin. In time she began praying for friends and employment. God met these needs through our student ministry, and then other students began praying with her. Now, five years later, Amelie has realized her dreams of becoming a French citizen, attending Bible college, and finding regular work. She's felt the touch of God in her life.

I share these things with you to give you hope and to show you how God transforms the lives of women who seek Him. If you desire to move beyond superficial living to explore the inner sanctuaries of the spiritual realm, I want you to know that there's more to life than this shallow world we live in. Experiencing God intimately is not exclusively for spiritual giants and saints like Mother Teresa or Billy Graham.

God desires ordinary people—people like you and me, people who have normal jobs and normal lives, people with resources and those struggling to get by—to trust Him and know Him in a personal way. He wants us to experience Him in the midst of ordinary activities and everyday relationships, in good times and in difficult times, in suffering and in joy.

The spiritual life can seem elusive at times if you were not brought up in a home where faith was revered and practiced as a way of life. The examples of spirituality can be confusing in our culture, where "anything goes" and so many paths are presented to us through the media and secular education. Growing up in a home with two religions, I found it baffling to try to figure out which message to embrace and whom to trust.

I have witnessed this phenomenon on college campuses time and time again. Many young women leave the routine and familiarity of home and begin to search for deeper answers to life's questions.

Becky and Tricia were both science majors at the University of Denver. These girls had their academic future by the horns, but they also had the stirrings of childlike faith. Both came from divorced homes and were deeply affected by their parents' poor and sometime volatile choices. For them, college was the chance to explore questions they could

> *"As the deer pants for streams of water, so my soul pants for you, my God. My soul thirsts for God, for the living God."*
>
> —Psalm 42:1–2, TNIV

never ask their parents. After I spent several months meeting with them, inviting them to a dorm Bible study and larger Christian gatherings on campus, both girls decided to place their faith in Christ. Their smiles showed the new confidence they were experiencing through intimacy with Christians and security in a heavenly Father and an eternal home.

To get to the place where I am today, I needed to get my feet wet, spiritually speaking. I needed to step out in prayer and start believing, and it was much like entering a pool and learning to swim for the first time. At first it felt like spiritual dog-paddling, but then my strokes got longer and more effective. Over time, I learned that there are spiritual disciplines that enable us to experience God more fully. These free us from fear, a need to control, despair, anxiety, and a selfish preoccupation with ourselves and the material world.

> *"Prayer catapults us onto the frontier of the spiritual life."*
>
> —Richard Foster,
> *CELEBRATION OF DISCIPLINE*

I've learned that when I am free from all that weighs me down, that which imprisons me in a joyless existence, I can experience new levels of joy and a deeper awareness of God's presence.

These may be new concepts for you, but I am willing to go out on a limb and tell you that God is calling you to deeper and fuller living. It's time to put away our desperate attempts at living in a make-believe world of perfectionism. Only He is perfect, and we are foolish when we try to be so.

Let's acknowledge, at the same time, that inwardly we long to live a life of adventure, meaning, risk, and drama. We are tired of a life of caution and shallow activity. We are tired of letting our past hurts and disappointments cripple us with anxiety, stress, and confusion. We want to take hold of the glimpses of a life lived hand in hand with the Creator of the universe, our Abba Father, who can help us live the life we've always dreamed of. We don't need to listen to the lies that run through our heads anymore—lies that tell us that we are desperately alone, that we can't trust anyone, that we must fight for what we want in life.

Spiritual transformation does not come about by sheer willpower or the right attitude. We can't make ourselves more spiritual or live more noble and godly lives. It's an act of grace.

Grace originates with God and is not "produced" by our own initiative or based on personal merit. Therefore, the changes we are most desperate to experience must come directly from God and His work in our lives, not our own. Grace is a gift from God.

SPIRITUAL DISCIPLINES

Over the ages, God has revealed the disciplines of the Christian life as a way to allow us to experience His grace on a daily basis. History shows, through the example of millions of Christians throughout the world, that these disciplines by themselves can achieve nothing. We experience transformation through humble faith and surrendering our will to God. God can take our patterns, anxiety, and stress, and change us over time by indwelling our lives and transmitting His power through our words and actions—even our feelings and desires. There are many helpful books written about spiritual disciplines. I find that the most vital disciplines for me are prayer, reflection, study, worship, confession, fasting, and service. If you are new to such things, let me offer a brief explanation of each.

PRAYER is simply talking with God. It is the surest and most direct way to relate to Him. You can speak with God in all honesty and expect His transformation in your life, trusting Him for His provision and protection. (John 15:7, James 4:3)

REFLECTION is tuning out the noise of the world to focus on God. It's meditating on God and the life He's called us to live as a part of His kingdom. (Ps. 46:10, 63:6, 145:5)

STUDY requires investing time in God's Word. It's purposefully studying the Scriptures in their proper and historical context, applying them to our everyday lives. (Ps. 119:9, 11; Phil. 4:8)

WORSHIP is opening our hearts to the love of God. It can involve meeting together with other believers, prayer, Scripture reading, confession, communion, service, tithing, and singing to God in an attitude of praise. (Matt. 4:10, John 4:23, Heb. 13:15)

CONFESSION is laying bare our inner lives, fears, worries, and obsessions, and admitting our sins to God. It includes asking God to help us turn away from our selfishness and thanking Him for His forgiveness. It may require asking for His help to overcome addictions or harmful behaviors, or to reconcile with loved ones. It means avoiding the things or relationships that cause us to sin. (1 John 1:9, 1 Pet. 2:11)

FASTING is abstaining from food for spiritual development. It's a private matter, and it helps believers focus on God and their spiritual life rather than the distraction of eating. Fasting can also apply to any other object or activity (television, shopping, dating) that may come between you and God. Some people fast for one meal; others fast for as many as forty days. (Matt. 6:16–18)

SERVICE is the act of submission, mercy, and goodwill toward other people in the name of Christ. It may include evangelism (telling others about Christ) or helping the poor and downcast. Christian service can involve teaching, financial gifts, hospitality, counseling, the arts, and many other forms or gestures. Service is not concerned with earthly rewards or status. (Matt. 20:25–28, Gal. 6:2, Eph. 4:11–13, 1 Pet. 4:9)

You can practice all of these spiritual disciplines simultaneously or focus on just a few at a time. What motivates me is the genuine desire to stay close to God and to receive His grace. Deuteronomy 7:9–14 says, "Know therefore that the Lord your God is God; he is the faithful God, keeping his covenant of love to a thousand generations of those who love him and keep his commandments ... therefore, take care to follow the commands, decrees and laws I give you today ... He will love you and bless you ... more than any other people" (TNIV).

In a stressful and highly competitive world, it gives me peace of mind to know that I'm not alone and that my life counts for eternity. God sees me and is intimately aware of my greatest needs. He wants to bless me and illuminate my life with His beams of light. He wants to bless my children and their children. He knows my dreams and has even bigger plans for me than I could ever imagine. Most of all, He loves me unconditionally.

YOUR SPIRITUAL JOURNEY

Remember Ellen, the young mother at the beginning of the chapter who found herself questioning her marriage and sense of personal fulfillment? It wasn't long after she began praying, in her own simple way, that God began to reveal Himself to her more intimately. Through a part-time job she found to take her mind off her predicament, she met an older woman who began to share with her the hope she had in Jesus Christ. This woman's example became Ellen's spiritual compass. She needed to trust God with her fears and uncertainties about her marriage and her new role as a mother.

Before long, Ellen began attending church with her co-worker and meeting other women who bolstered her confidence and showed her how to love and enjoy her family.

Time spent with these women who loved God and served actively in their churches and communities helped Ellen look at her life with new eyes. Yes, there were still occasional struggles with her husband and their age difference, and at first he didn't support her growing spiritual interests—he was afraid of losing her. But as she learned to be patient and focus on the positive aspects of their family life, Ben began to trust her more. Ellen found a routine that worked for their family, and Ben gave her the support she desired to continue to develop spiritually.

Some women may experience conflict in their dating relationships or marriages when they are not at the same spiritual level as their partner. They may have a greater desire to mature spiritually and be involved in church life than the men in their lives. Some may even aspire to go into full-time ministry, attend seminary, or go on a short-term missions trip.

If you're single, choose carefully the kind of men you date. Dating often leads to marriage, and the potential for heartache is great if you choose a life partner who does not appreciate the things you value spiritually. Never go into marriage thinking you can change your husband. If the guy you are dating is not interested in your faith, chances are high that he won't be interested later on, either. I know too many women who feel trapped in spiritually dead marriages. No amount of gentle prodding or manipulating will change a man's heart spiritually. It's an act of grace and requires his personal faith.

Some women have a great need to perform acts of Christian service or to use their intellect for God's glory. If you are seriously contemplating greater involvement in your church life, going to seminary, or entering into full-time ministry, hold off on dating guys who don't share the same interest. Move in the direction of your spiritual interests and trust that God will bring the right relationship to you once you are actively engaged in your desired realm.

In college, I rarely dated. Even though I enjoyed the liberal nature of my education and made friends easily, I didn't share much in common with many of the guys I sat next to in class. I had a sense that God would lead me to a serious dating relationship once I completed my studies and began my vocation in full-time ministry. In my case, this mindset paid off. I was engaged to my husband sixteen months after graduation. I was fortunate to meet him—he had many of the same spiritual convictions and interests—halfway around the world while serving with a college ministry. Maybe God has the same kind of thing in mind for you.

As women, sometimes our spiritual life doesn't take off until we become mothers. Then, the challenges of raising children drive us to our knees and push us through the doors of a church. We want the best for our kids and willingly make sacrifices in order to give them every advantage life offers. As the moral bearings of our society become shaky, we crave the help of other people in raising our kids.

> "A woman who understands what is true, right, and lasting creates and establishes a home for her husband and family where security, encouragement, and peace dwell."
>
> —Cynthia Heald, LOVING YOUR HUSBAND

Rachel started thinking more about God when her four-year-old daughter, Emma, began asking questions about how life began. Rachel dusted off some Bible stories she remembered as a child but felt guilty that her answers seemed to fall flat. She hadn't been to church since her sophomore year in high school and didn't relate much with churchgoers. Emma's questions caught her by surprise but made her realize she would probably need to address the issue more deeply in the years to come.

One day a neighbor stopped by Rachel's house with a bag of used children's books that her own children had outgrown. Inside, Rachel found nearly a dozen books about the Bible written for preschoolers, along with other books about Disney characters and the ABCs. Hungry for answers to Emma's spiritual questions, Rachel began reading the Christian books every afternoon to her daughter until Emma seemed satisfied about the nature of God and His creation. Not long afterward, Rachel realized the Bible stories had made an impression on her own heart. She started talking to God in prayer before she feel asleep at night and asked her neighbor about her faith. A new world opened up to her.

Like Rachel, many young mothers begin to grow spiritually by sharing their questions with a neighbor or by visiting a church, Bible study, or prayer support group. Whether they do it for themselves or their children, sooner or later they feel a connection with God and other believers. Motherhood opens their eyes to new possibilities and new relationships they may have never entertained before. Now they want to be a part of a greater story.

You may be thinking, *This sounds like my life, but my husband is not there yet.* If so, let me encourage you to remain patient and joyful. Try not to let your husband's lack of spiritual interest drag you down or threaten your marriage. Know that your faith provides a spiritual covering over your family (1 Cor. 7:14). If you remain positive, faithful in prayer, supportive, serving, and loving, your husband's heart may soften, and he may adopt your faith or give you the freedom to practice as you like.

The man who is antagonistic or cruel to his wife usually feels threatened. He fears losing control of his marriage and family. Or he's afraid that being spiritual is less manly. Let your husband's attitude and behavior be a barometer of how much time and energy you devote to church activities. It's better to go about your spiritual interests quietly and progressively rather than disrupting your marriage and family routine. Give it time, and place your trust in God (1 Pet. 3:1–6).

Perhaps you are ready to take your life to the next level spiritually. You are tired of observing from the sidelines. You want to influence the world positively and be a spiritual-change agent. There are so many opportunities for young women to grow and serve in the spiritual realm. But it's not always easy to decide how involved to be at church, in our communities, and in our vocation when we have so many other commitments elsewhere. If you desire to devote more of your time to expressing yourself spiritually, let me offer some suggestions.

1. BEGIN PRAYING. Ask God to reveal His wonderful plan for your life. Be honest with Him about your passions, and ask Him to give you direction for the future. Pray that He brings the right combination of people and experiences into your life to make the right choices. Consider even going away for a weekend to pray and fast about the matter. Seek to hear God's voice.

2. SPEND TIME WITH MATURE BELIEVERS. Ask a lot of questions and feel free to express any hesitations. Tell them about your growing desires and ask if they have any advice.

This may be your best source of contacts and referrals later on.

3. RESEARCH YOUR AREAS OF INTEREST. If it's missions, go on a short-term (two- to six-week) mission project. If it's seminary, take a class online or at a local Bible college. If it's working with a church, ask to lead a Sunday school class or help out administratively to get your feet wet. Talk to people who are already in ministry. Begin making specific goals to achieve your spiritual aims.

4. EXECUTE. Take the initiative to begin living out your goals. Take whatever steps are necessary to make your dreams a reality. Inform your parents or family members. See yourself as a minister of the Gospel in whatever capacity you choose. Trust God's promises of provision as you begin to understand your new role.

In an age filled with anxiety and stress, isn't it comforting to know we have a God who loves us deeply and wants to bless us with His grace and love? We no longer need to live perfectionist and controlling lives characterized by fear and suspicion at every turn in the road. Yes, we will still struggle—after all, we are human. But we don't need to drive ourselves over the edge of sanity because of an illusionary world of status, beauty, and power. God created us in His image, and we can derive no greater value than being His children and living according to His will. Let's find confidence, like those who have gone before us, in the simple but profound truth "that the chief end and duty of man [and woman] is to love God and to enjoy Him forever."[3] Nothing else can truly satisfy, so why not—in hope, faith, and love—lay down our boxing gloves, get out of the ring, and get on with our lives as they were meant to be lived?

ONE OF THE FOLLOWING ORGANIZATIONS MIGHT BE A GOOD FIT FOR YOU:

ACTION AGAINST HUNGER
www.aah-usa.org

AFRICARE
www.africare.org

ATHLETES IN ACTION
www.aia.com

BRIDGES INTERNATIONAL
www.bridgesinternational.com

CAMPUS CRUSADE FOR CHRIST
www.ccci.org

CARE
www.careusa.org

CHILDFUND INTERNATIONAL
www.childfundinternational.org

CHRISTIAN CHILDREN'S FUND
www.christianchildrensfund.org

COMPASSION INTERNATIONAL
www.compassion.com

DATA
www.data.org

FELLOWSHIP OF CHRISTIAN ATHLETES
www.fca.org

FEMINISTS FOR LIFE
www.feministsforlife.org

FRONTIERS
www.frontiers.org

GLOBAL HOPE
www.globalhope.org

HABITAT FOR HUMANITY INTERNATIONAL
www.habitat.org

INTERNATIONAL JUSTICE MISSION
www.ijm.org

INTERVARSITY
www.intervarsity.org

MEDAIR
www.medair.org

NAVIGATORS
www.navigators.org

PRISON FELLOWSHIP
www.pfm.org

SAMARITAN'S PURSE
www.samaritanspurse.org

WOMEN FOR WOMEN INTERNATIONAL
www.womenforwomen.org

WORLD RELIEF
www.wr.org

WORLD VISION
www.worldvision.org

YWAM
www.ywam.org

Chapter 9

EMERGING FEMININITY: HOW THEN SHALL WE RAISE OUR DAUGHTERS?

"We are being given the illusion that women can accomplish anything today and that it is her fault if she does not."

—SIMONE DE BEAUVOIR

We are the third wave of feminism, whether you realize it or not, and we're at a crossroads characterized by narcissistic liberalism and crushing conservatism. We're living a pressure-cooker existence, trying to be all things to all people—successful, beautiful, godly, financially secure, faithful wives, committed mothers. We're standing on the shoulders of the women who came before us, as early as the 1700s—women like Sarah Grimke, Judith Sargent, Catherine Booth, Susan B. Anthony, Sojourner Truth, even Simone de Beauvoir, Betty Friedan, and Gloria Steinman. We may not agree with all their ideas or the liberties they have fought for, but our lives have been altered from previous generations nonetheless. They have handed us many of the rights and privileges we too often take for granted, and in many respects, some of the freedoms have created for us a whole new set of problems.

We are the generation now looking around and asking what choices we should hang on to and what falsehoods we should cast aside. Sometimes it's incredibly confusing. We want to do all the right things, but aren't always sure how—most of us are building our lives from scratch, and sometimes it is a scary and lonely place to be. Baby-boomer women are rarely available. They are too busy with their careers and with caring for aging parents, or are too self-preoccupied to help us move into the future. Will it be any different for our daughters' generation?

> *"Confusion and shame often reign ... Half the world wants to have a baby, but it's an insipid, sexist throwback to say that starting a family is a goal in life."[1]*
>
> —Julie Manenti

Who do we listen to? Feminists or traditionalists? The reds or the blues? Naomi Wolf or Nancy Leigh DeMoss? If we choose to stay home full-time and bake cookies, the Left tells us we are losers. If we choose to work outside the home, even on a part-time basis, and rely on childcare, the Right tells us we are nearly criminal.

Some of us tell ourselves that if we can juggle the right number of balls, we can live in both worlds. Balance. But it's never that easy. Most mothers instinctively and inevitably shore up for the rest of the world and double up as caretakers at the end of the day.

Some of us do a better job than others of tuning out the static—we are free agents and figure out arrangements with our husbands that give us higher levels of freedom and creativity in our marriages. I think of my cousin Diane, who teaches at a university two nights a week and homeschools, which includes lots of fun extracurricular activities and socializing with her children during the day. Despite his macho athletic and hunting prowess, her husband teaches sixth grade, cooks (he makes a killer clam chowder), and enjoys sharing the parental load. For me, they are the definition of the millennial couple, and she is the definition of emerging femininity.

But most of us, if we are truly honest, are hoping and praying that we are making the right choices while we carry the lion's share of the domestic work, with little time for ourselves. We are desperate for a future less riddled with anxiety and stress. Even though we hear from well-meaning female leaders in media and politics that we don't need to compromise our independence in marriage or motherhood, we know the concept is trickier than it appears. Most women who make such promises don't have children yet or are rich enough to afford full-time nannies. But what about the rest of us? What will we tell our daughters about their future someday?

THE NEXT GENERATION

A time will come when we will have to be honest with ourselves and future generations that modern female life is still a bumpy road with a lot of potholes—a far cry from the sleek autobahns you'd find outside of Berlin or Paris that the second wave of feminists promised us in the 1970s if only we'd believe in ourselves a little more. Today, women's issues revolve not so much around our rights or wants, but around how to live with the number of choices afforded to us. We are quickly coming to learn that every choice we make has an upside and a downside. As Danielle Crittenden shares in her book, *What Our Mothers Didn't Tell Us*,

> We must understand the tradeoff of every action we
> take. If we want to be heart surgeons or presidents, we

will have to accept that we may not be the mothers we want to be, or may not be mothers at all. If we are unwilling to trust men, we might not have the marriages we want. If we refuse to give ourselves over to our families, we cannot expect much from our families in return. If we wish to live for ourselves and think only about ourselves, we will manage to retain independence but little else.[2]

Let's face it. The mixed messages our daughters are getting are being etched onto their souls. This is the season, as Maureen Dowd so picturesquely describes, "when the ideal is not Gloria Steinem, a serious bunny, but Jessica Simpson, a simple bunny, when Hollywood's remake of *The Stepford Wives* stumbled because it was no longer satire but documentary."[3] In fashion magazines, on television, and on the Internet, the computer-generated, airbrushed female clones are our daughters' role models—not educated women who want to help change the world and care about education, the poor, and the rights of the minorities.

In many respects we have come full circle; women are trapped by the modern notions of sex, dating, marriage, and financial success. With our society's obsession over appearance and materialism, our growing reality is a future where men prefer hot zombies to smart career girls, where homes are quickly approaching the million-dollar mark, and where children must be superstars.[4]

DATING, SEX, AND MARRIAGE IN THE NEW MILLENNIUM

At some point or another, we'll have to tell our daughters that women may have "found themselves," but they have also lost something in the process—deep and meaningful relationships. Let me paint you a picture of your daughter's future.

PROBLEM NUMBER ONE: A growing number young females are outpacing males in education. Male college enrollment is falling behind that of females.[5] We have pushed our girls academically and vocationally, in hopes of greater liberties and individuality, but their future as happy wives and mothers looks bleaker than ever. Researchers are reporting that women with higher IQs have a lower chance of getting married (even though it remains an asset for men).[6] These kinds of trends show that highly educated women, particularly those with postgraduate degrees, are increasingly dealing with domestic non-choice by delaying marriage and childbearing.[7] If men don't start catching up and suddenly find smart young women attractive, our daughters may very well look back on their education and career goals (often driven by their parents' dreams) as a cruel hoax.

> *"New links must be forged as old ones rust."*
>
> —Jane Howard,
> WRITER

PROBLEM NUMBER TWO: *The New York Times* reported in 2004 that "men would rather marry their secretaries than their bosses, and evolution is to blame."[8] Meanwhile, the University of Michigan ran a study among college undergraduates that suggested that men who want long-term relationships would rather marry women in subordinate jobs than women who are their supervisors.[9] Men are apparently threatened by women with more powerful jobs because they fear that sooner or later, these women will cheat or walk out on them. Who would have guessed the male ego is so fragile? Like it or not, this is our daughters' future.

PROBLEM NUMBER THREE: Economist and author of *Creating a Life: Professional Women and the Quest for Children,* Sylvia Ann Hewlett conducted a survey in 2002 that reported that 55 percent of thirty-five-year-old career women were childless. In addition, 49 percent of female corporate executives who made $100,000 or more did not have children, as compared to only 19 percent of men. Hewlett went on to say, "The rule of thumb seems to be that the more successful the woman, the less likely she will find a husband or bear a child. For men it is the reverse."[10] Wow! Looks like the feminist notion of sexy, powerful careers has turned out to bite us in the rear.

If these statistics don't unnerve you and you're still hopeful that your little straight-A daughter will snag a great guy sooner or later, let me warn you that it may be a lot harder for her than it was for you. Times have changed, and I'm witnessing the trends firsthand as I work among college students and young professionals. It's getting tougher and tougher for young women between eighteen and thirty-five to meet decent guys who will commit. It's possible that at some point, the dating pool for women will be filled with divorcés or widowers.

I know feminists insist that marriage should not be the end-all for women—the blue ribbon, so to speak, for all our hard work. But the truth is, most people desire it and are happier when they are married. Psychologists can tell you that married people live longer, are less depressed, have fewer addictive and financial problems, and are less involved with crime. Sure, there are smart and successful single women doing just fine on their own, but most would tell you that deep down, they'd love to share their lives with another.

I realize some readers may think this line of reasoning sounds old-fashioned, even countercultural, but after living on three continents and working in a profession in which I hear about people's greatest needs and longings, I can tell you that your daughter may very well desire marriage sooner or later, and you must be ready to engage in this interest with her. You must be prepared to plan with her and support her in a world where relationships between men and women are becoming increasingly more complicated for educated and successful females.

We'll have some tough questions to answer in the years to come. Like, how do we help our daughters pursue their educational and vocational goals *and* find a lasting marriage and motherhood? How will we help them communicate with their husbands and support their need for a life outside of the home when motherhood alone does not satisfy?

One of my goals in writing this book was to give readers a chance to think about their identity and plan for the lives they want to live, instead of just accepting the possibility of a bleak future. The more information you have on the front end, the less anxiety and confusion you'll experience once you start hitting the life stages and struggles I discuss in this book. My hope is that you will feel less alone or isolated, and a little less crazy or depressed when life doesn't turn out the way you expect.

The second thing I wanted to accomplish was to create a cultural conversation, to get young women exploring their insecurities and feelings. I'm hoping the conversation might even become cross-generational, that young adult women will ask their mothers or older female role models about their own struggles and fears and dreams and passions, and learn how they work

> *"The Second Wave (feminists in the 1970s and 1980s) did their work—not particularly well—and now we are stuck with a bucket-load of unsolvable problems."*
>
> —Tamara Straus,
> "LIPSTICK FEMINISTAS"

through many of the same issues. After all, our quest for better self-esteem, beauty, love, and godly heritage is certainly not new to this millennium. So call your friends, get together, and start talking about the things that strike a chord in you.

CAREERISM'S BACKLASH

As a now-motherless daughter, I question a lot of the presuppositions I've had about modern female life. Even though I lost my mother in junior high, I still had relatives and friends who pushed me academically and vocationally. They also had high standards materialistically. They wanted my generation to become doctors, lawyers, engineers, and educators. Many of my peers have their master's or doctorate degrees, or are at the top of their fields. While I respect the high standards they have passed on to me, I sometimes question where we've all ended up. We may be "successful" by the world's standards, but divorce and broken relationships clutter our generation's landscape. Many of us are living independent and lonely lives and increasingly few are having children. And if we do have children, we only choose to have one or two, and then thrust them into the care of nannies or daycare workers. There's nothing wrong with childcare, but it feels like something has been lost in the thirst for career success and independence among my female cohorts. I'm left asking, "Have we, in our male-centered thinking, forfeited the gift we've been given as females to create life and to make a home feel like home?" Is it too late to teach our own daughters differently?

THE COST OF WAITING

In addition, I've noticed a great number of females who put off marriage and/or motherhood until their thirties and forties but are now struggling with no marriage prospects, shaky marriages, or infertility. And I'm not the only one who has noticed this trend. In her book, *Gender: Men, Women, Sex and Feminism*, Frederica Mathewes-Green comments on this increasing phenomenon:

> A pattern of late marriage may actually increase the rate of divorce. During the initial decade of physical adulthood, young people may not get married, but they're still falling in love. They fall in love, and break up, and undergo terrible pain, but find that with time they get over it. They may do this many times. Gradually they get used to it; they learn that they can give their hearts away, and take them back again; they learn to approach a relationship with the goal of getting what they want, and keep their bags packed by the door. By the time they marry, they may have had many opportunities to learn how to walk away from a promise. They have been trained for divorce.[11]

Green has a point here. Serial dating and avoiding marriage seem to set young people up for bigger problems down the road. We end up looking for the phantom ideal. We try to convince ourselves that Mr. Right is out there if we'd just keep looking. So we keep dating or remarrying, hoping we will find "that special someone" sooner or later, as if marriage is about getting rather than a mutual-love relationship.

Meredith is thirty-one and still single. She leases a Mercedes-Benz and rents a 1,200-square-foot apartment in Laguna Beach. She works out three times a week and gets her hair highlighted once a month. Besides her full-time job at an attorney's office, she is working toward her realtor's license. Most women envy her because she's sexy, smart, and dates regularly—but never one guy for more than a few months. She's looking for someone, she says, who can offer her the kind of life she wants to live, who has the "cool factor," who has enough money so that she can stop working someday and have as many kids as she wants.

Meredith may not represent your life or your daughter's life completely. But aren't we all a little like her in some way or another? Aren't we all still looking for our Prince Charming on some level?

Let me tell you a hard truth: he's not out there. I've been working among young women for more than a dozen years, and I don't know too many who would say they married anyone remotely close to their idea of Prince Charming. Yes, we have great husbands who love us and want the best for us—but none are Prince Charming with a 5,000-square-foot villa and a Lamborghini parked out front. We stand by our men because we believe in a greater story. We believe in the permanency of marriage and family and in the gift we can give our kids by keeping our marriages together. We choose to love even when it's not convenient because we believe it matters. That means children need their dads just as much as their moms.

> *"American women are among the freest and most liberated in the world. It's no longer reasonable to say that as a group women are worse off than men."*[12]
>
> —Christina Hoff Sommers,
> AUTHOR

We're doing the next generation a disservice if we keep feeding them unrealistic expectations for their future. Girls who invest their hard-earned energy to go to the best colleges and snag the best careers are no more certain of getting the best husbands than those who settle for a lot less. Maybe our model of female success and catching the right guy is upside down. Rather than pushing our kids to get their MBAs and holding out for Mr. Right, maybe we should provide equal support if they desire to begin building their lives earlier rather than later. Maybe we should begin talking with them about the realities of married life and motherhood in their teens and twenties instead of waiting for them to come cry on our shoulders when they are overwhelmed or depressed in their thirties and forties.

Most of us blanch at the thought of our children marrying under the age of twenty-five ... the immediate reaction is, as Mathewes-Green says, is

> "They are too immature." We expect [them] to be self-centered and impulsive, incapable of shouldering the responsibilities of adulthood. But it wasn't that way through most of history ... most of us would find our family trees dotted with teen marriage ... it's hard for us to imagine such a thing today. It's not that young people are inherently incapable of responsibility— history disproves it—but that we no longer expect it.[13]

RAISING OUR DAUGHTERS WITH THEIR EYES WIDE OPEN

In my case, I was the first to marry among my high-school and college friends. I graduated from college, went overseas for a year, met my husband, and married a year later at the tender age of twenty-three. Some of my relatives and friends may have raised their eyebrows, but I knew in my heart that I had found my soul mate. To be honest, I had considered breaking up with him after we'd been together for six months to continue "dating" again, just in case there was someone better out there. I remember sitting on my bed one afternoon, "considering my options," when I believe God spoke to my heart. He opened my eyes to my double standards and selfish thinking. He revealed to me how Clyde met so many of the dreams I had for a husband and that if I walked away from the relationship, there was no guarantee I'd ever meet someone like him again. It was as if God were shining a bright searchlight on Clyde, saying, "This is the man I've prepared for you."

As mothers, we must speak to our daughters openly about the realities of adult female life and teach them how to communicate their true desires for marriage, motherhood, and vocation. Such open discussions should never be taboo or laughed at. We must speak to them about the realities of rapid changes in male/female relationships when women start to take more leadership roles in society. We must encourage them not to have unrealistic expectations about the kind of man they might marry and how they will "balance" their careers with family life. We can avoid the anxiety and stress so many in our generation have suffered if we talk about these things earlier rather than later.

Most importantly, we must teach the next generation that we can't escape the consequences of our choices and actions. Yes, we want our daughters to be accomplished, to make the most of every opportunity, to express their talents and gifting—but not at the loss of their God-given femininity. When all is said and done, we must teach our daughters never to define feminine success and independence on male terms (whether socially, sexually, or vocationally) but by female ingenuity. Think of it as originality within a female framework. We must find womanly ways of expressing ourselves and living in community. Perhaps there are even new frontiers, new businesses, new educational fields that will remain unexplored until we stop trying to live and work like men, and start living

I never thought this day would come,
When I was thinking about life when I'm thirty and some.

Just shy of sixteen, and a whole life ahead,
There are many lives to choose; at least that's what
I've read.

Each day it is different for what I will be,
Pop star singer, famous nurse, or just plain fully me.

There's the job of a mom, complete with a van,
Or a model like woman, on the prowl for a man.

I want to be beautiful; I want to be known,
Or be like the woman I've always been shown.

A balance in between of the two that I see,
An exceptional life changer, that's the woman I'll be.

This woman is radiant, yet stunningly real,
It's compassion and love that fill her with zeal.

As a woman I look toward the future ahead,
I'll follow the life she vivaciously led.

—Danica Kushner,
NINTH-GRADER

and working like women.

Our girls need to know that we can't—and shouldn't try to—live men's lives. In fact, maybe if we didn't have so many women trying to live like men, we wouldn't have so many stressed-out, control-freak "alpha moms"—one of the lovely byproducts of our hyped-up times. Women who look like they are on steroids or need Ritalin, and who, as Maureen Dowd describes, "are armed with alpha SUVs, which they drive in an alpha overcaffeinated manner ... equipped with their alpha muscle from daily workouts and alpha tempers from getting in the teachers' faces to propel their precious alpha kids."[14]

> *"To be somebody, a woman does not have to be more like a man, but has to be more of a woman."*
>
> —Sally E. Shaywaitz,
> PEDIATRICIAN AND WRITER

Rather, let us move forward and teach our daughters that life is simpler than we make it out to be. Relationships are the key to happiness, not status, financial security, or material things. Not even writing books or some other dream job. Let's teach them to revere marriage and family life so much that they work to live, rather than live to work. To love people and use things, not use people and love things.

Whether or not you are a mother, you will need to take an honest look at your own family background. It's okay to admit that your family situation wasn't perfect. If you are unsure about the kind of mother you will someday become or about how you are doing today, know that God sees you. He loves you and wants the best for you and your family. He wants to bless you and affirm you. He knows your history and wants to help you build your life in a way that promotes healing and gives you hope for the future. Perhaps you will have to examine some wrong or naive assumptions you have about married life or motherhood. Maybe there are some myths you will need to put to death. Maybe there are some dreams you will have to lay at His altar.

Trina is a single mother of two teenage daughters. She never went to college because she got pregnant at the age of nineteen, and has been burned in several relationships with men. Now that her daughters are blossoming into young women, she is telling them to "go to college, become doctors, be independent, and don't think about marriage unless someone 'good enough' comes along."

While I agree that education is extremely important for our daughters, I'm saddened that Trina is pushing her girls toward autonomy and painting such a negative picture of men, as if they are the root of all of our problems. Perhaps men took advantage of Trina, but it doesn't mean they have to take advantage of her daughters. With the right kind of planning and boundaries, they can both accomplish their educational goals and meet great men who will make fine husbands someday.

Young women don't need to grow up believing that men will block them from their dreams and that they should put off marriage and motherhood as long as possible. Trina's pain doesn't need to repeat itself in two young girls who find themselves successful but desperately lonely someday.

As I think about what's important to tell our daughters as they plan for their future, I've come up with some suggestions I'd like to share with you.

TALK OPENLY ABOUT HOW GROWING TRENDS IN EDUCATION AND CAREERS PLAY OUT IN MALE AND FEMALE RELATIONSHIPS. Inquire about the level of your daughter's desire to marry and have children as early as possible. If she's extremely maternal, help her form educational and career goals in a manner that will allow her to marry and have children with greater ease. If she's extremely ambitious vocationally, discuss with her the growing tendency of singleness among highly educated and career-driven women. Either way, she should plan for her future with her eyes wide open.

MODEL FOR YOUR DAUGHTER HOW TO TRUST GOD FOR DREAMS AND GOALS. Cultivate a strong work ethic tempered with humility and grace. Talk about the pressure today's young women feel to be successful, beautiful, and in control of their lives. Help her to understand what things make her anxious and stressed, and show her how to cope with the pressures of our society. Teach her that godliness isn't measured by actions, but by the state of our hearts, our attitudes, and our ability to experience peace and hope amidst difficult situations.

HELP HER TO APPRECIATE MODESTY, BUT NOT AT THE EXPENSE OF SACRIFICING A SENSE OF PERSONAL STYLE. Tell her that true beauty is not measured by the examples of computer-generated or airbrushed women on the cover of magazines. Explain that media and advertising often play on our insecurities to get us to buy their products. We can feel beautiful when we take care of our bodies and allow God's light to emanate from within.

EXPRESS TO YOUR DAUGHTER THE NEED TO RESPECT MEN AND NOT LOOK TO THEM TO SOLVE THEIR PROBLEMS. A husband is a life companion, not a financial broker. She should not expect him to make all of her dreams come true financially or materialistically. Husbands want to love us and protect us, but there's no guarantee they'll give us everything we want in life. Instead, God wants us to come to Him for our deepest longings, in an attitude of faith and humble submission.

DEMONSTRATE FOR YOUR DAUGHTER THE FEMININE ART OF HOSPITALITY, OF MAKING A HOME "FEEL" LIKE A HOME. Cook together, fold laundry together, garden together, arrange flowers together, put on makeup together, entertain together, visit the sick together ... show her acts of kindness and service to guests. Teach her to be a lady.

ENCOURAGE HER TO FEEL COMFORTABLE WITH AND LOVE CHILDREN. Help her find baby-sitting jobs. Model for her how to speak to children or care for babies. Tell her that one of the greatest gifts God has given her is to create another life. Elevate motherhood to its rightful place of honor.

TELL HER THAT SHE DOESN'T HAVE TO SACRIFICE HER PERSONAL LIFE ONCE SHE HAS CHILDREN. It's good for kids to see their moms being creative and entrepreneurial, volunteering, or serving others outside of the family. It will look different for every woman, but each of us is entitled to express to our husband and children the need to have a hobby or work outside of the home.

TEACH YOUR DAUGHTER TO LEARN WHEN SHE NEEDS TO REST AND MAKE TIME FOR SOLITUDE. When she's tired and irritable, give her permission to close the door and take a nap or spend time reading or daydreaming. Pray with her. Take quiet walks with her. Go on a silent retreat with her. Buy her a journal. Show her how to listen to her body and spirit and find refreshment in Christ.

Chapter 10

MENTORING THE NEXT GENERATION OF ANGELINA JOLIES

*"The time is ripe for a new movement—a seismic holy
quake of countercultural women who dare to take God at
his Word, those who have the courage to stand against the
popular tide, and believe and delight in God's plan
for females."*

—MARY KASSIAN,
The Feminist Mistake

When my son was eight months old, I arranged for an
American girl to come live with my family for a couple of
months so I could enroll in a full-time French program in
Paris. I desperately needed to learn the language to survive in
our new life in Europe. Anna flew from her home in Texas
and settled into our little 800-square-foot apartment. What
a trooper! It was cramped, but we made it work. I left baby

Quinn with Anna from eight thirty in the morning to four o'clock in the afternoon every day. In the evenings we cooked dinner together, learned about each other's lives, and hung out. Some of my friends thought my husband and I were crazy to have a young woman living in our tight, two-bedroom apartment, but we loved the arrangement. Sure, we could have hired a babysitter during the day, but I liked the idea of having a young female be a part of our family experience—partly because Anna allowed me to finally delve into the language with more focus, but mostly because we loved being around students and young adults. We cherished the opportunity not only to influence and mentor the next generation, but also to grow in new ways ourselves.

> *"It is better to light a candle than to curse the darkness."*
>
> —Eleanor Roosevelt

We have had more than a dozen girls—whom I met through my ministry work—live with us in the United States and in Europe. The thing I treasure about having a younger woman in my home is that it forces me to look at the world a little differently. I am always amazed by the things they have to teach my children or the way my kids respond around them (more behaved). It's as if we all work a little harder to get along, and this then becomes a habit. What always blows me away is how God uses this time in the young woman's life, too. Each has remarked about something new she learned or how God spoke to her of new possibilities.

When they go home, we get phone calls and emails from their parents asking, "What did you do with my daughter?! She's so positive and helpful. She's excited about so many new things ... she's a woman!"

There's not much I can say, other than that I treated their

daughter like an adult. I looked her in the eye, and I took an interest in her life. I gently prodded in areas that needed prodding and encouraged her to live with integrity. I spoke openly about my convictions and personal interests. I also shared my own struggles and doubts. I hope they see that even though I am not perfect, I love people and want the best for them. I like to help women see their lives through the lenses of potential and vision. I have no formula, and it looks different with every new girl who comes to stay with us, but God always shows up and does something special in their lives.

Nelleka from Holland became a fashion designer. Andrea from Denver is a research scientist. Sara from the Middle East created an interactive website for a large European ministry. Ruth from Seattle is on missions trip in Africa. Mariska from Holland is a new wife and mother. Katie from Baltimore is traveling the world by ship with Semester at Sea. Adeline from Paris is helping with a local church there. Elisabeth from Denver is a near-genius high-school student. She has spent the last two summers with us and has taught my kids a ton of great brain-teaser games and ways to engage in "adult conversation." She's also volunteered in my husband's media department and has one of the most mature relationships with God I have ever witnessed in a woman under the age of twenty. These are just a few of their names and some of their stories.

So why do I keep opening up my home every summer, spending money on extra groceries and outings and baby-sitting? Because I see how spending a little extra time with a young woman can have a huge impact on her life. These are the women of our future. They will work in education, the arts, science, and the business sector. They will get married someday and have children. They will be the pillars of their churches and their communities. And we don't just hang out together. I put them to work. They help with baby-sitting and get involved in our home life. They attend church with us and help me entertain guests who come into our home. I also encourage them to volunteer as a part-time intern at my husband's workplace, whether with college students or in media, in order to get some work experience. The arrangement seems to work well, and everyone seems to enjoy each other in the end.

These are the same women who are saturated every day by mixed message about their identity. They live real lives and have real struggles, like any other woman their age. They have good parents who love them and who, for the most part, attend church, but that doesn't mean they don't question who they are and grapple with how to develop their own personal goals and dreams. These are females who are torn between a biblical and a secular worldview. They long for beauty and significance, but also for healthy and godly families someday. These are women who need the freedom to ask questions and not feel pressure from family or church to conform to a certain standard or regimen. They are individuals and need to know that God sees them and has given them certain talents and gifts to use for His kingdom. The hard part is figuring out how to get there.

That's where I come in. I am interested in their lives and like to dream with them. I can ask questions that parents or other people may be afraid to ask. How's your relationship with your boyfriend, really? If you are making mistakes, what changes can you make? What are your dreams, and what would you do if you could do anything at all? Where do you want to travel in the world? How do you want to blend marriage, motherhood, and/or a vocation someday? What are your fears? Why are you so hard on yourself? How can you take better care of yourself? What is God saying to you right now?

The conversation flows naturally over dinner and while washing dishes, folding laundry, taking the kids to sports events, and heading over to the beach for the day. We talk about my writing and media projects and how I juggle work with family. We pick up where we left off the day before. Most of all, we have time to linger and talk about things on a deeper level than most people are able to because we are together for an extended period of time.

Whatever they observe or learn from my life is genuine, in the context of real living. You can't hide much when you live under one roof. It's not like meeting a mentor for coffee once a week, sharing goals and prayer requests. They see me in my jammies in the morning, with mascara smeared under my eyes. They see me when I get cranky with my kids or disagree with my husband. They also see how I care for a family and still pursue my personal goals outside of the home. They see me close the door and write for two hours a day. They see how I spend my money. They hear how animated and passionate I get when I talk about people I love, or the ministry I am involved with, or the things I still hope to accomplish someday.

> *"The critical responsibility for the generation you're in is to help provide the shoulders, the direction, and the support for those generations who come behind."*
>
> —Gloria Dean Randle Scott,
> PRESIDENT, BENNETT COLLEGE

They look at my life and see a woman who's a little further down the road than they are, and they see that it's going to be all right. They can still have a life. They can still have vision and passion. They can still enjoy primping and talking about "girlie stuff." They can have a loving husband and great kids and lofty dreams and an eternity with their Maker. They can see into the future, and that gives them life.

YOU CAN MAKE A DIFFERENCE

What about you? You may be thinking, *I have never mentored anyone before in my life. And I am only nineteen or twenty-nine! Who am I to bring someone into my home, even on a weekly or part-time basis, and pour into her life? What can I offer? I don't have enough life and work experience.*

It doesn't take an expert or someone with a PhD to begin mentoring women. Young women all around us are desperate for genuine and authentic friendships. They want to know someone has taken an interest in their lives and desires to help them plan for the future. They want to know that someone believes in them and sees their potential. They want a sounding board for their fears, insecurities, hopes, and dreams. They want someone besides their parents and pastor to go to with their hard questions. They want someone to give them some honest feedback, even if it's painful or requires changes in poor habits or relationships.

I realize you may not be able to—or even desire to—let another young women move in with you or your family for weeks at a time. But there are lots of ways this kind of a relationship can begin once we feel the stirring to influence another woman's life.

The relationship can develop slowly over time. Invite her over for meals or spend the day together. Ask her to spend the weekend or the holidays with you. Include her on a family vacation or a spontaneous overnight trip, perhaps over Christmas or spring break, during a spiritual retreat, or for a special project at church or in your community. Most of all, do what's natural for you and the relationship.

You don't need special books, materials, or training—just a little bit of space in your life and in your heart. If you are not sure how to begin, pray and ask God whom He may have in mind. Look around your church or workplace. Maybe it's a niece or younger female relative. Maybe it's the daughter of a co-worker. Maybe it's a young mother in your neighborhood. Just keep your heart open.

I remember living in Paris and seeing a certain woman pass under my apartment's kitchen window each day as she walked her kids to school. I decided to pray and ask God to help me meet her. Finally, I introduced myself to her one day at our children's preschool. It turned out that we were both pregnant and due the same day. Six months later we were friends, eagerly sharing our hospital delivery stories and introducing our baby daughters to each other. Three years later, she cried in my arms when we left Paris.

THE NEXT GENERATION OF ANGELINA JOLIES

I am fascinated by Angelina Jolie, even though it's nauseating sometimes how often I see her image in the grocery-store checkout line. Not because I love gossip magazines or because she's drop-dead gorgeous or because she snagged Brad Pitt from Jennifer Aniston. She reminds me of so many girls I meet these days. Girls who've come on our summer missions project in Paris, or as exchange students who volunteer with Habitat for Humanity in Mexico or Global Hope in Afghanistan. These are women, churched and unchurched, who have a growing hunger to do what's right, even if they don't live like saints or haven't figured everything out yet. Angelina certainly doesn't have a pristine track record, and maybe the wool's been pulled over my eyes, but I sense from her humanitarian work and adoptions of third-world children that she loves people and cares about the poor and oppressed like few of her Hollywood peers.

I wonder who her role models are. Who inspired her to want to help the disenfranchised and marginalized, to sacrifice her personal comfort and safety to go to some of the most dangerous places in the world, and to adopt babies no one else wants? My travels have taken me to enough of the same remote places to show me that it is not as glamorous as it looks on the cover of *People* or *In Touch*. I hope it's not a publicity stunt. I am inclined to believe she represents a growing trend among young women who want to live lives that make a difference in the world. They are willing to take risks and overcome taboos. They are not afraid of AIDS and interracial families. They are tolerant of people of other cultures and religions, even if they don't embrace the same spiritual beliefs.

How many other "Angelina Jolies" are out there today? With a little bit of love and direction, they could turn this world upside down. I wonder what kind of personal and spiritual choices someone like Angelina would make if she had women in her life who pointed her to Christ. Maybe she'd be with Brad Pitt, or maybe she wouldn't—that's not the point. She'd be an instrument of God, and she'd be serving Him for the good of the world. She'd raise up an army of other like-minded women to work alongside her, and she'd inspire couples to do the same. She'd encourage people to take care of orphans and AIDS victims with grace and dignity. She'd be the jewel of everyone's eye.

> *"When so rich a harvest is before us, why do we not gather it? All is in our hands if we will but use it."*
>
> —Saint Elizabeth Ann Seton

But instead, she's living her life backward, and her reputation is being dragged through the mud. She's the subject of every gossip magazine. People love dirt, and they love finding it in her life. Her past mistakes, which would normally be kept secret, are uncovered daily. We know about every tattoo on her body and every lover since high school. She's a living target for greedy paparazzi types and our insatiable appetite for gossip and titillating news. With all of her fame and fortune, she's a celluloid tragedy in the making, rather than a radiant star.

Who are the little Angelina Jolies in your life? What role could you play to help them embrace their dreams and God-given abilities, without the attack of the world and the dangers of bad choices and bad press? Who are the young girls in your life who need someone to talk to, to share with, to ask questions—who simply need to feel loved and valued? Who are the women desperate for significance, beauty, security, and a legacy? Who are the females who have that special spark in them, who you can tell want to take the world by the horns? What steps can you take toward them to let them know you are available to listen to their dreams and concerns?

I hope that if Angelina Jolie or others like her ever get ahold of this book, they'll know there are women out there who care about them. We see their vision and their passion, and we want to come alongside them. We want to be available to be a sounding board and to pray for them. We want them to know their dreams aren't crazy; they are God-given. Most importantly, their lives matter to God. Christ died for them, and the world desperately needs them to do what God has put on their hearts.

Go ahead, pick up the phone and invite that special young woman over for a cup of tea. Be real and invite her to do the same. Better yet, have a party and invite some young girls over for a fun meal. Don't be shy. Take a risk. Ask good questions. Listen. Share your own stories. Pray together. Open the Word together. Volunteer together. God may give you the chance to influence a future leader, the mother of a child, the wife of the next president, a teacher, a missionary, an artist, a filmmaker, a neighbor, a co-worker, another human being.

MENTORING IN PRACTICAL WAYS

• *Visit her campus or workplace and have lunch together.*

• *Be a good listener.*

• *Ask her about her childhood and religious background.*

• *Invite her to spend a day or weekend with you.*

• *Remember and celebrate her birthday.*

• *Discuss her career path and specific vocational goals.*

• *Go window shopping together and learn about her tastes.*

• *Focus on personal and spiritual development.*

• *Show affection.*

• *Allow her to see you be real and vulnerable.*

• *Spend time outdoors together.*

• *Plan a creative dinner party together with some of your friends.*

• *Ask about her views on marriage and motherhood.*

• *Gently point out harmful patterns, like exhaustion, insecurities, and bad relationships.*

• *Invite her on a spiritual retreat with other women.*

• *Suggest helpful books about spiritual formation and female identity.*

• *Go to the movies and talk about the film afterward.*

• *If she's dating, go on a double date together.*

• *Praise her and speak openly about the things you admire in her life.*

Final Musings

When I first shared about this writing project with a friend, she challenged me on the book title. "How could you possibly write a book about wanting all the right things?" she asked, as if she thought I was getting in over my head or might breed discontent among young women who don't have or can't have what I want. While I respected her thoughts, I realized that there is a lot of fear among women today regarding our different priorities and lifestyles. The culture war is felt so deeply among us that we are threatened when some women make choices that are different than ours. It challenges our self-esteem, and we want to avoid as many casualties as possible.

At the same time, my intention with this book has never been to tell women what their insecurities and desires are, but to help them identify them. I want to help give women the freedom to express their struggles, to be open with each other, and to explore solutions for a life with more hope and joy. I want to help women make the right choices, both individually and corporately, in ways that impact their communities for good and point them toward Christ.

Feminist Betty Friedan died the week I completed this book. Although I don't agree with all of her ideas, I am indebted to women like her—women who are incredibly intelligent and dare to speak their minds and reveal what's in their hearts. I want to be more like that. Through her book *The Feminine Mystique*, she created a cultural conversation for women who instinctively know that something isn't quite right about their modern lives. She wrote, "It was a strange stirring of dissatisfaction of yearning that women suffered in the middle of the twentieth century ... each suburban wife struggled with it alone ... and she was afraid to ask even herself the silent question, is this all?"

Today we take for granted the changes and freedoms Friedan and her predecessors ushered in for us. Our problems are different but felt just as deeply. As *The Washington Post* writer Ellen Goodman describes, "Today *Desperate Housewives* is a television show. Mothers at home still bristle at [Friedan's] description of their 'dissatisfaction.' Four decades later we have mommy wars and arguments about educated women, 'opting out' of work. Women with Fortune 500 companies can also ask, 'Is this all?'"[1] So the conversation must continue.

I am neither a feminist nor a traditionalist. I love thinking about women's issues and have more to learn from both camps; I see the value of blending the two worldviews. I tell my friends I am conservative when it comes to raising my children, but liberal in the realm of ideas, future possibilities, art, and cultural expression. Like a coat of many colors, I'm a mixture of values, traditions, and ideals, with Christ at the helm of my life. I am a part of a new movement best described as emerging femininity.

I recognize that the women's movement came with many problems—namely, that our "freedoms" have meant that our stock is lower than ever with men, and we are hurting ourselves every day sexually and emotionally by trying to behave like another gender. We have a long way to go before we are truly liberated and comfortable with our femininity. The revolution is unfinished.

But traditionalists don't hold all the keys to happiness and fulfillment, either. The Victorian arrangement they prescribe doesn't work for all women or all couples. More and more couples must learn to submit to one another in reverence to God (Eph. 5:21), with a mutual appreciation for our unique creation as men and women. We need to be careful not to identify too closely with either group. As Naomi Wolf, author of *The Beauty Myth*, says, "We need more dialogue between feminists and faith communities—the discussion enriches both." Emerging femininity means we must listen carefully to and empathize with women's needs, pointing them to solutions that benefit not only themselves but their families and communities. For me, it begins with a personal relationship with Christ and trusting that He can speak to each woman in her unique station in life.

I've come to learn that there is no formula for a woman's life or the Christian life. We all have different talents, gifts, energy levels, histories, cultural backgrounds, passions, temperaments, finances, families, and interests. We are each uniquely created. The only constant is God and His Word.

I am also a student of people and desire to help women make sense of their lives. I have dared to challenge readers with things we keep private but ache to share with each other. I have been open about my spiritual perspective. Only through spiritual lenses can we begin to grapple with our true identity and our deepest longings, and plan for the lives we so desperately want.

When we take our needs and desires to God, we can be assured that He wants the very best for us (Matt. 6:25–34). He cares about what we care about. He isn't concerned if we are fifteen pounds overweight. He doesn't care what kind of car we drive, whether we have a 401(k), or the color of our kitchen walls. He cares about our passions and insecurities. He cares that we keep our heart focused on Him. We are precious to Him, and the dreams we have are not mere coincidences— He will use those to draw us closer to Him and reveal His will to the world around us. He is with us in everything.

My prayer is that throughout this book, I have articulated some feelings you have experienced in private but haven't talked about openly yet. Hopefully I have given you some insight as to why we struggle the way we do and have offered some helpful advice. Some of the things I've shared may seem subversive, even a little risky. I am not afraid to be countercultural. And I hope you aren't, either.

I know I've only scratched the surface, in some respects, and there is so much more I could write—but that wasn't my goal. There are a lot of excellent books out there that deal with women's issues, singleness, marriage, and motherhood. There are women's classes you can take and female leaders you can speak with. I have shared one perspective. You have the ability to dig deeper, talk to your girlfriends, and find the mentors you need.

Why?

Because you're smart, resourceful, and thoughtful. In a lot of ways you are more comfortable in your skin than I am. I have lived and worked among enough students and young professionals to know that I have things to learn from you, and I hope I have been able to pass on a few things to you as well. Wherever you are, know that you have a soul sister who cares about you, prays for you, and wishes she could sit down with you over a cup of coffee and talk about your questions and worries, your dreams and passions, or just shoot the breeze. Maybe someday, in Paris or New York or Los Angeles. Hopefully we will meet each other soon. Who knows what the future holds? I believe in you. The best days are ahead of us.

Questions for Reflection

CHAPTER 1:
WHAT NO ONE EVER TOLD US

1. Describe the areas of adult female life you feel unprepared for. What do you wish you had been told about earlier, to prepare for the transitions you are going through now?

2. How would you describe your relationship with your mother or an older female role model? Is she able to give you satisfying answers to questions about adult female life, marriage, motherhood, female friendships, and vocational pursuit? If not, whom can you turn to?

3. How would you rate your ability to navigate the mixed messages you receive from liberal feminism and conservative traditionalism?

4. How do magazines and television messages shape your identity, spending habits, and worldview? How do you discern what's true and what's fabricated?

5. If you are a wife or a mother, what is your level of anxiety, fear, and loneliness? What do you wish you could change about

your situation? What is the first thing you would change about your life or schedule?

6. How has your education or religious upbringing affected the way you see your life as a woman, wife, and mother? In what areas of your life do you feel feminism has benefited you? How has it let you down?

7. How can the Church be more effective in helping young women intersect their faith with culture and domestic life?

CHAPTER 2:
DESPERATE FOR SIGNIFICANCE

1. There is a big difference between a need to live a life of significance and to simply be a success? How would you define the difference?

2. What compels you to pursue your dreams and goals with dogged determination? If you feel like you are always climbing uphill and getting distracted, what barriers do you need to overcome? How can you find more support?

3. Make a list of five to ten of your dreams. Rank them in order. What can you accomplish this year, and how?

4. How has your upbringing affected your view of significance? How does God define a life of significance?

5. What mixed messages do you receive from feminists or traditionalists about what it means to be significant as a woman? How do you discern what messages are right for you?

6. Name a few of your role models who have lived a life of significance. What attributes characterize their lives? What can you learn from them?

7. How do goals and accountability help you experience the level of significance you desire? Do you prefer to work alone or in a group? Whom can you turn to for advice in reaching some

of your goals?

8. If you struggle with perfectionism, what goals or dreams may be more about "proving yourself" than about something that brings you pleasure and invigorates you? What things do you need to let go of? What does God want you to trust Him for this year?

CHAPTER 3:
DESPERATE FOR BEAUTY

1. Who has influenced your views of beauty and why? Your mother? Your peers? Advertisers? Celebrities?

2. What aspects of today's beauty standards are most difficult for you to achieve? Do you ever feel like you can't measure up? Why?

3. Name the role models in your life who practice stylish modesty. What makes them appear beautiful or attractive to you? What can you learn from their example?

4. Do you feel like you have been subtly influenced by the pornography industry to question your own personal beauty, your figure, or your style of clothing? Do you feel like you need to have a more shapely figure to attract men and be respected by your peers? Have you thought about getting implants? Why? What are the potential downsides?

5. Do you struggle with your weight? Are you attracted to pictures of celebrities who are nearly anorexic? How do you reprogram your mind not to buy into the message from the advertising industry that you need to be as thin as a rail? Where can you find support to live a healthy life and feel good about the body God has given you?

6. Do you think singles or marrieds struggle more with beauty issues? Why? How do you feel about aging? How can

you prepare now for the aging process, to ensure that you will feel good about yourself in the years to come?

7. In what ways can the Church help young women dealing with beauty insecurities? How can the Church equip women to better translate the mixed messages they receive about modesty and developing a sense of personal style? How can we better support women who struggle with their weight or self-esteem?

SUGGESTED READING:

In Pursuit of the Ideal, Nancy M. Wilson

Captivating: Unveiling the Mystery of a Woman's Soul, John and Stasi Eldredge

The Beauty Myth: How Images of Beauty Are Used Against Women, Naomi Wolf

Why Beauty Matters, Karen Lee-Thorp and Cynthia Hicks

Loving Your Body: Embracing Your True Beauty in Christ, Deborah Newman

Eve's Revenge: Women and a Spirituality of the Body, Lilian Calles Barger

---

CHAPTER 4:
DESPERATE FOR INTIMACY

1. Are you enjoying deep and meaningful friendships? Why or why not?

2. Describe your best friends or soul mates. How do these people make you feel about yourself? How do they energize you? What have you learned from them about being a friend?

3. If you have moved recently or anticipate moving, how can you make new friends? Where do you like to meet new people?

4. When or where is it hardest for you to initiate with new people? Do you ever feel like you have to beg for friendships or sell yourself? If so, how does this affect your self-esteem and trust in people?

5. If you feel lonely or left out, whom can you talk to? A relative? A pastor? A neighbor? Are you willing to take a risk and share about your loneliness with an acquaintance and see how God works in that situation? Are you willing to trust Him for a new friend?

6. How do you relate to older women? Is it hard to find things in common? Do you think you would enjoy friendships with older women? If so, whom do you have in mind, and how can you initiate the relationship?

7. Do you sense a competitive nature in your relationship with other women? Is it easier for you to relate to men? What makes you feel threatened or insecure in your relationships with women? How can you overcome these barriers?

8. What kinds of women do you need to avoid because they affect your self-esteem poorly or encourage bad habits?

CHAPTER 5:
DESPERATE FOR SOLITUDE

1. Do you frequently feel fatigued and drained? Why? Do you give yourself permission to rest or get to bed at a decent hour?

2. How many hours of sleep do you need to feel rested? Are you often able to achieve this amount? Why or why not?

3. What does solitude look like for you? Describe the perfect locale to experience solitude and silence. How do you find pockets of silence during the day?

4. What do you like to do by yourself? Read? Journal? Draw?

Shop? Garden? Do these activities energize you and help you re-engage in life again? Do you feel you enjoy your family and friends more after you've been able to pull away and spend some time alone?

5. How many books do you read a month? A year? If you are not reading on a regular basis, why not? What would you like to read next?

6. When is it most difficult to make time for yourself? How can you express to your spouse or roommate your need for some alone time?

7. How do you make time for God in your life? Where do you like to pray and open the Bible? How can you cultivate a listening spirit in your life through moments of solitude? When or where is it easiest for you to hear from God?

CHAPTER 6:
DESPERATE FOR FINANCIAL SECURITY

1. Describe your relationship with money. Do you operate from a position of scarcity (somehow you never seem to have enough) or from a position of abundance (somehow you always seem to have more than you need)? Does spending money stress you out or energize you?

2. When does the need for financial security border on selfish greed? What is the difference? How do you know when your needs or desires are merely a form of coveting what others have?

3. What are your greatest financial fears? List the things you want to trust God for in the coming year. What about the next three to five years?

4. Do you find it difficult or easy to keep a budget? Why?

5. Who are your financial role models? What have you

learned from them?

6. In what ways do you look to men—whether your father, husband, or boyfriend—to provide for you financially? What ideas are based on feminism or traditionalism? How can you trust God rather than an ideology?

7. Do you feel pressure from society to have certain things? If so, what? Which of these are truly essential, and which are illusions of wealth?

CHAPTER 7:
DESPERATE FOR A LEGACY

1. How has your view of motherhood been shaped? Who are your role models?

2. What are you thoughts on shared parenting? Is it really possible? How does your husband or boyfriend feel about it? Or do you prefer to be the main caretaker? If so, why?

3. What are some special experiences you want to share with your children? What are some things you'd like them to experience that you were not offered as a child?

4. Describe some positive things your parents modeled for you. How can you pass these on to your children?

5. What are your greatest fears about parenting children in our generation? Where can you find support to help raise your kids the way you want? Church? Relatives? Neighbors? Certain kinds of schools?

6. What are some of the negative effects of media you see in children these days? How can you protect your kids from these negative elements? How can you speak frankly with them about these things, without invoking fear or rebellion?

7. Do you trust God for your children's future? If not, what steps can you take to do that?

8. How can you avoid the "motherhood religion" (treating your children like idols) and the need to control every area of your children's lives? How are you preparing your children to enter adult life as godly, loving, and responsible citizens?

CHAPTER 8:
DESPERATE FOR THE SUPERNATURAL

1. Describe your spiritual background or history. How did your parents raise you spiritually? What were the positive and negative aspects?
2. Do you have a need to experience God personally in your life? If so, describe the things you want to trust Him for and how you want to experience Him more fully.
3. In what ways do you find it most difficult to trust God? What are some personal fears or anxieties you need Him to attend to?
4. What steps can you take to develop more intimacy with God? If you are not already in the habit of practicing Christian disciplines, which ones would you like to begin this week? This coming year?
5. Who are your spiritual role models? What spiritual biographies or books would you like to read? Whom can you turn to for spiritual guidance?
6. What kind of long-term personal ministry would you like to develop? How can you begin researching this area of interest? Whom can you talk to about your desires and goals?
7. What kind of spiritual heritage do you hope to pass on to your kids? What spiritual practices do you wish to experience or share as a family? How can you encourage your husband or boyfriend to develop a devotional life with you?

CHAPTER 9:
EMERGING FEMININITY:
HOW THEN SHALL WE RAISE OUR DAUGHTERS?

1. Describe your relationship with your daughter, niece, or a special young girl in your life. What dreams do you have for her? What kind of relationship do you hope to have with her in the next five to ten years?

2. What values or life lessons do you hope to pass on to her? What positive aspects of feminism or traditionalism do you want to share with her? What falsehoods do you want her to avoid?

3. Describe your views on dating and marriage. When will your daughter be old enough to marry? How do college and career fit in?

4. What are your views on premarital sex, and what will you tell you daughter? What are the benefits of waiting until marriage? Is it possible? Who are her role models?

5. How can you help your daughter plan for the future? How would you explain blending motherhood with a career (even on a part-time basis)?

6. Based on your daughter's vocational ambitions, what advice would you offer about choosing a husband?

7. What marriage stressors should your daughter be aware of before tying the knot? Finances? Infertility? Materialism? In-laws? Children's education?

8. What things can you do now to help your daughter plan and prioritize for the future?

CHAPTER 10:
MENTORING THE NEXT GENERATION OF
ANGELINA JOLIES

1. Describe your favorite role models or mentors. If you have never been mentored, share what kind of a mentor you'd like. Where can you find this kind of person?

2. How do you feel about mentoring a young woman? Does it scare you or make you dream about possibilities? Whom do you wish to initiate with first?

3. What kinds of life experiences do you have to offer younger women? How can you relate to their modern challenges or insecurities? What lessons would you like to pass on?

4. What are some practical ways you can meet the needs of the women in your spheres of influence? Meet for coffee or lunch? Go shopping or redecorate their apartment? Baby-sit for their kids? Loan them good book to discuss later?

5. Does a mentoring relationship have to be structured or can it be a way of life? What are the benefits of both? Which do you prefer and why?

6. What kinds of younger women are you drawn to? Students? Young professionals? Co-workers? Neighbors? Artists? Academics? Women in politics? Women at church? How can you begin initiating with these kinds of women?

7. How could your family benefit from your involvement in the lives of people outside of your home? What lessons could your children learn? How might it help shape their future or expose them to new possibilities?

NOTES

INTRODUCTION

1. Cathi Hanauer, *The Bitch in the House: 26 Women Tell the Truth About Sex, Solitude, Work, Motherhood, and Marriage* (New York: Perennial, 2002), Introduction/XV.
2. Judith Warner, "Mommy Madness," *Newsweek*, February 21, 2005.
3. Ibid., 44.

CHAPTER 1: WHAT NO ONE EVER TOLD US

1. Ibid.
2. Maria Elena Fernandez, "Men love their 'Housewives,'" *Los Angeles Times*, November 12, 2004.
3. Ibid.
4. Ellen Goodman, "Redefining marital happiness," *The Boston Globe*, March 17, 2006.
5. Rebecca M. Groothuis, *Women Caught in the Conflict: The Culture War Between Traditionalism and Feminism* (Eugene: Wipf and Stock, 1997), 2.
6. Ibid., 4.
7. Sandra Tsing Loh, "A Gloom of One's Own," *Atlantic Monthly*, October 2004.
8. Danielle Crittenden, *What Our Mothers Didn't Tell Us: Why Happiness Eludes the Modern Woman* (New York: Simon and Schuster, 1999), 184.
9. Ibid., 180.

CHAPTER 2: DESPERATE FOR SIGNIFICANCE

1. *Newsweek*, October 24, 2005.
2. Damah Film Festival: Spiritual Experiences in Film (*www.damah.com*).
3. Stephen King, *On Writing: A Memoir of the Craft* (New York: Scribner, 2000).
4. "How I Got There," *Newsweek*, October 24, 2005.
5. Ibid.
6. Judith Warner, *Perfect Madness: Motherhood in the Age of Anxiety* (New York: Riverhead, 2005), 176.
7. Brenda Hunter, *Home by Choices: Raising Emotionally Secure Children in an Insecure World* (Sisters, OR: Multnomah, 1991), 171.
8. Ibid., 171.
9. Groothuis, 213.
10. Peg Tyre, "Smart Moms, Hard Choices," *Newsweek*, March 6, 2006.

CHAPTER 3: DESPERATE FOR BEAUTY

1. Maureen Dowd, *Are Men Necessary?: When Sexes Collide* (New York: Putnam, 2005), 40.

2. Maureen Dowd, "What's a Modern Girl to Do?," *The New York Times Magazine*, October 30, 2005.

3. Myrna Blyth, *Spin Sisters: How the Women of the Media Sell Unhappiness—and Liberalism—to the Women of America* (New York: St. Martin's Griffin, 2004), 87.

4. Naomi Wolf, *The Beauty Myth: How Images of Beauty Are Used Against Women* (New York: Harper Perennial, 2002), 5.

5. Kristin Tillotson, "Liberation gone wild: Why are women exploiting themselves?," *Minneapolis Star Tribune*, December 18, 2005.

6. Susan B. Anthony paved the way for the Nineteenth Amendment, which gave women the right to vote. Her belief in God and in the equality of women made her a symbol of personal progress in America and around the world.

7. I am not against thongs. I just don't think women should openly display them in public (or above their pants line). Thongs are a sex symbol to men. When men notice a woman is wearing a thong, they may think she is advertising that she is sexually open to their advances. We need to take responsibility for the messages we send men with our clothing. We must respect that they see the world differently than we do and avoid putting ourselves or other women in dangerous or embarrassing situations.

8. Peg Tyre, "Fighting Anorexia: No One to Blame," *Newsweek*, December 5, 2005.

9. Ibid.

10. Dowd, "What's a Modern Girl to Do?"

11. Wolf, 283.

12. Blyth, 293.

13. Betty Blake Churchill, *Fantasy: An Insatiable Desire for a Satisfying Love* (Orlando: CRU Press, 2005), 110.

14. Ibid., 117.

15. Wolf, 286

16. Churchill, 110.

17. Blyth, 43.

18. Karen Lee-Thorp and Cynthia Hicks, *Why Beauty Matters* (Colorado Springs: NavPress, 1997), 237.

CHAPTER 4: DESPERATE FOR INTIMACY

1. Hunter, 145.

2. Warner, 220.

3. Ibid., 193.

4. Ibid., 23.

5. Susan Miller, *After the Boxes Are Unpacked: Moving On After Moving In* (Wheaton, IL: Tyndale House Publishers, 2000), 88.

6. Daniel Pink, "Revenge of the Right Brain," adapted from *A Whole New*

Mind: Moving from the Information Age to the Conceptual Age (New York: Riverhead Books, 2005).
7. Miller, 99.
8. Kirsten, Mary, Diane, Leslie, Janine, Susan, Jill, Shirin B., Robin, Sonya, Susane, Marsha, Lisa, Alisa ...

CHAPTER 5: DESPERATE FOR SOLITUDE
1. Warner, 165–166.
2. François de Salignac de La Mothe Fénelon, *Let Go: To Get Peace and Real Joy* (New Kensington: Whitaker House, 1973), 9.
3. Richard J. Foster, *Celebration of Discipline* (San Francisco: Harper and Row, 1978), 95.
4. Bill Bright, *A Handbook for Christian Maturity: Ten Basic Steps Toward Christian Maturity* (San Bernardino: New Life Publishers, 1992), 129.

CHAPTER 6: DESPERATE FOR FINANCIAL SECURITY
1. Claudia Wallis, "The New Science of Happiness," *TIME*, January 17, 2005, A5.
2. John Gottman, *The Seven Principles for Making Marriage Work: A Practical Guide from the Country's Foremost Relationship Expert* (New York: Three Rivers Press, 1999), 194.
3. Wallis, A5.
4. Ibid., A6.
5. Research based on University of California psychologist Sonja Lyubomirsky's findings, as reported in "The New Science of Happiness," *TIME*, January 17, 2005.
6. Wallis, A4.

CHAPTER 7: DESPERATE FOR A LEGACY
1. Warner, 191.
2. Blyth, 115.

CHAPTER 8: DESPERATE FOR THE SUPERNATURAL
1. Jennifer Barrett, "Capturing The Sound of Silence," *Newsweek*, January 23, 2006, 10.
2. Foster, 1.
3. The Westminster Catechism.

CHAPTER 9: EMERGING FEMININITY: HOW THEN SHALL WE RAISE OUR DAUGHTERS?
1. As quoted in New Voices, an editorial forum for readers under thirty (*Orlando Sentinel*, April 8, 2006).
2. Crittenden, 189.

3. Dowd, "What's a Modern Girl to Do?,"11.
4. Ibid., 42.
5. Laura Fasbach, "The Gender Gap: Women's dominance has schools courting males," *Knight Ridder-Tribune News,* January 31, 2005, *http://www.journalnet.com/articles/2005/01/31/features/isu01.txt.*
6. Dowd, "What's a Modern Girl to Do?," 47.
7. Ibid., 54.
8. Ibid., 53.
9. Ibid.
10. Frederica Mathewes-Green, *Gender: Men, Women, Sex, Feminism* (Ben Lomond: Conciliar Press, 2002),103.
11. Ibid., 100-101.
12. Christina Hoff Sommers, "Sex, Lies, and Feminism," speech at University of Chicago, January 2003.
13. Mathewes-Green, 104.

· FINAL MUSINGS
1. Ellen Goodman, "She Changed Our Lives," *Orlando Sentinel,* February 7, 2006.

[RELEVANTBOOKS]

FOR MORE INFORMATION ABOUT
OTHER RELEVANT BOOKS,

check out www.relevantbooks.com.